Thank … Fat…

W. Phillip Keller

WORD PUBLISHING

WORD (UK) Ltd
Milton Keynes, England

WORD AUSTRALIA
Heathmont, Victoria, Australia

WORD COMMUNICATIONS LTD
Vancouver, B.C., Canada

STRUIK CHRISTIAN BOOKS (PTY) LTD
Maitland, South Africa

ALBY COMMERCIAL ENTERPRISES PTE LTD
Balmoral Road, Singapore

CHRISTIAN MARKETING NEW ZEALAND LTD
Havelock North, New Zealand

JENSCO LTD
Hong Kong

SALVATION BOOK CENTRE
Malaysia

THANK YOU, FATHER

First published in the U.S.A. by Word Incorporated Dallas, Texas

First U.K. edition 1990, Word (U.K.) Ltd.

ISBN 0–85009–342–2 (Australian ISBN 1–86258–102–9)

Reproduced, printed and bound in Great Britain for WORD (U.K.) LTD., by Richard Clay Ltd., Bungay, Suffolk

Thank You, Father

BY THE SAME AUTHOR

Splendor from the Sea
As a Tree Grows
Bold under God—A Fond Look at a Frontier Preacher
A Shepherd Looks at Psalm 23
A Layman Looks at the Lord's Prayer
Rabboni—Which Is to Say, Master
A Shepherd Looks at the Good Shepherd and His Sheep
A Gardener Looks at the Fruits of the Spirit
Mighty Man of Valor—Gideon
Mountain Splendor
Taming Tension
Expendable
Still Waters
A Child Looks at Psalm 23
Ocean Glory
Walking with God
On Wilderness Trails
Elijah—Prophet of Power
Salt for Society
A Layman Looks at the Lamb of God
Lessons from a Sheep Dog
Wonder o' the Wind
Joshua—Man of Fearless Faith
A Layman Looks at the Love of God
Sea Edge
David I
David II
Sky Edge
Chosen Vessels
In the Master's Hands
Predators in Our Pulpits
Songs of My Soul
Thank You, Father

To
MY FATHER, IN HEAVEN
with genuine gratitude
for
His compelling companionship, His intimate care,
and His unfailing understanding upon the path
of life

Contents

Preface:

The Reasons for This Book

It is important for the reader to know why this book was written. It is imperative to understand the motives that brought it into being. It is helpful to grasp clearly what its objectives are.

First, it is a humble but sincere tribute to the honor and faithfulness of my Father, God. It is a memorial to His integrity and trustworthiness all through the recent years of my quest for His companionship.

Second, it is an attempt to show that even amid the so-called sophistication of our scientific society, an ordinary person can live and walk by faith in God, our Father. In the common details of life, He *does* demonstrate His unfailing care and love for the one who quietly follows Him.

Third, the book demonstrates that putting total reliance in our Father injects a dimension of delight and adventure into life that transcends the stress of our earthly sojourn. He brings beautiful bonuses into our experiences that inspire our spirits, quicken our souls, and energize our bodies.

Lastly, this story, if it can be called that, proves the living reality of my Father. He is here! Even though a skeptical society may deny His existence, He does reside with those who obey Him, who love Him and relish His company.

Chapter 1

Good Cheer for Tough Challenges

It was a joyous occasion. Ursula and I were married, very quietly, in a beautiful sanctuary whose great glass windows looked out over the ocean on one side and the mist-shrouded mountains on the other. It was a moving moment for us because the pastor who presided was a man of great vision for reaching all the South Pacific region with the good news of our Father's love.

He had aroused in us a willingness and desire to be a part of the response to such a thrilling challenge. This was years before contemporary society spoke so freely about the emerging economic might of the so-called "Pacific Rim Trading Region." He was a visionary twenty years ahead of his time. A man of great good will who had come to the Hawaiian Islands and there founded a flourishing work in the heart of Waikiki, he was one whose faith in God and great good cheer were a contagion for us as a couple.

Our first response to this challenge was to offer to do the basic, rough, tough pioneer work on a beautiful property he had acquired for a Christian camp. It was located on the Big Island of Hawaii, in a rather remote spot at the northern tip where the ancient, easy-going pace of the "Old Hawaii" still prevailed.

The day we drove into the site in our camper my spirit was subdued and still. The whole place—fields, gardens, buildings and roads—was literally buried in tropical brush. The relentless jungle of the windward slope, nourished with over 100″ of rain, was engulfing everything in green vines, rank reed-like grass and verdant jungle growth.

Where did one begin?
How does a man without equipment or tools
take on such a tough task?
Whence comes the strength, the
stamina, to carry on in this steamy
climate?

We parked our compact little camper just inside the gates. One could drive no further. Then we set out to explore the acreage. In former times it had been a substantial school for Hawaiian youth. But long ago it had been abandoned. Now great green creepers ran right over the rooftops. Their tentacles hung over the eaves, darkened the windows and even tried to grow into every crack and crevice around the doors.

Former formal gardens, walks and roads were lost to sight under a dense tangle of sprouting trees, tall grass and lush ground growth. The playing fields, once lying open to the sun, smiling at the sea below, were becoming themselves a sea of thick waving grass up to a man's belt buckle.

Everywhere there were insects: scores and scores of insects of assorted shapes, sizes, and stinging abilities. Their various webs, nests and offspring invaded not only the jungle growth outside but also occupied the various rooms inside. Spiders, huge creatures of brilliant hues, endless troops of ants and hordes of cockroaches had taken over the territory.

It was not the sort of spot for the faint of heart or weak in will to spend their honeymoon! But we had resolved from the outset that we would endeavor to serve the Master no matter where He led us. So in this jungle setting our first stiff challenge to trust Christ unflinchingly was met.

With a certain element of trepidation, co-mingled with quiet assurance that my Father would supply the strength to see us through, I went down to a nearby general store in search of tools. The portly proprietor was a huge Hawaiian lady of ancient Island stock. Her place was festooned with the assorted goods most in demand by the local people—fishing gear, garden tools, cooking utensils and basic dry goods, with a meager supply of simple foodstuffs.

I selected a sturdy axe, a hefty Mexican-style machete, two razor-sharp Chinese sickles and a cross-cut saw, along with a huge box of old-fashioned matches. The unusual purchases by a "hauli" (white person from the mainland) aroused the lady's curiosity. "Coming to live here?" she asked in a rough tone of voice. Tourists were welcome. Permanent residents who might occupy some of the precious land were not!

"Just for a few months," I replied casually. "I've come to restore the old school site again and make it a beautiful place to benefit other people." Her face brightened as she gave a sigh of relief. "I will need help, so if you know anyone expert at clearing jungle please send them over!" With that I left.

Though as a young man I had cleared a lot of land in Canada, in the prime of my strength, those days were long past. I was now well beyond middle life with only moderate vitality which drained away under the equatorial heat and humidity of Hawaii. A few hours of heavy labor cutting creepers, slashing grass and chopping down trees left me soaking with sweat. My rough work clothes clung to my frame. My heart pounded. And by midday I was ready to drop.

Then one morning a battered old jeep, splattered with mud, came into camp. The driver was a tough looking little man of Filipino origin. His face was deeply lined; his skin was wrinkled like ancient leather; he appeared even older than I except for one thing. He possessed a certain tough, whipcord vitality that aroused my admiration.

He could speak only broken English. I knew little of the local lingo in which the co-mingled races of Hawaiians, Chinese, Samoans, Filipinos and other Pacific Islanders communicated. But I did come to finally understand (using sign language and facial expressions) that he was offering to help me. What I did not know was that my Father had clearly heard my plea for strength and stamina. Here before me stood a bundle of energy, expertise and humble loyalty bound up in a simple soul of great good will.

His name was Lino . . . short, sturdy, to the point, just like the man. With uncanny intuition he sensed exactly what needed to be done. He could almost read my mind, even if he could scarcely understand my speech. He seemed eager, ready, glad to get going on the job which was as much a challenge to his skill and strength as it was to mine. "Thank You, Father!" I exclaimed within my spirit. "We will win!"

A few days later Lino brought a friend—the sturdy fellow might have been his twin. So suddenly there were three of us tackling the task. At 6:15 A.M. sharp, Lino would rumble up the road. Fifteen minutes were spent sharpening all the tools. Then at 6:30 sharp, clearing would commence. Relentlessly the chop-chop-chop of machetes and axes rang through the trees. The slash-slash-slash of sickles cut through the reeds, grass and vines.

We accumulated huge piles of underbrush. Soon Lino showed up with jeeploads of old truck tires. Using these to fuel the fires, we soon had roaring infernos burning up all the debris, even in the pouring rain (that would have quenched most land-clearing operations).

For most moderns who apparently have unlimited money, machinery and manpower to get a job done, our endeavors may have seemed pretty commonplace. But for me it was an extraordinary demonstration of how one man with unshakable confidence in his Father could see His hand at work.

As a youth my dad had instilled in me a sturdy concept of cooperation with God. This concept has never left me. It is summed up in two simple lines:

"I WILL DO MY BEST,
MY FATHER DOES THE REST."

Using every ability and energy at my disposal, I would do my utmost to achieve His purposes upon the planet. Beyond that I could, in quiet faith, trust my Father to supply the resources and achieve the end through other men and means He made available.

Lino was a case in point. Though worlds apart in culture, nationality, language and traditions, we were drawn into a unique bond of affection, loyalty and mutual respect seldom seen. We were like brothers caught up together in a common cause.

Swiftly, surely, steadily, week by week we pushed back the jungle. The grounds began literally to glow with sunshine falling upon the close-clipped lawns. The trailing vines were torn from the buildings that stood shimmering in the sunlight again. The paths, walks and roads were cleared. Opened to traffic, they once again provided pleasant places to walk. The fields were opened up, mowed and lay green with new-cut grass against the blue of the Pacific beyond.

In all of this exciting advance Ursula played her part in supplying lovely trays full of fresh fruit, refreshing cool drinks and delicious fruit salad. It was no easy thing for her to be camped in a spot where spiders strung their webs over the bushes and even over the shower stalls; where cockroaches had set up permanent residence in every crack and pipe in the place; where hordes of ants marched down the paths, across the floors, up the walls and even into the camper. Despite such drawbacks we often relished quiet times of love and laughter together.

Suddenly in the midst of all this our Father sent us further delightful allies: the local birds. To our unbounded delight every square yard of ground we gained was immediately taken over by our feathered friends. All sorts of birds moved into the clearing. They just loved the newly cleared fields, the graveled paths, the open spaces beneath the trees where they could feed and fly freely as in a park. They made vast inroads on the insect population. Literally angels in disguise, they did a clean-up job far better than any we could accomplish.

The birds did even more than that. They brought a glorious aura of beauty, song and pure pleasure to the place. The flash of their wings, the brilliant hues of their plumage, the warbling notes of their calls, the cooing of the doves on the paths, injected an element of peace and contentment into the whole camp.

As month followed month even we were happily surprised to see how beautiful this spot had become. I had taken a series of photographs both before and after our efforts. It hardly seemed possible so much could be accomplished in such a short time by so few.

One other exotic bonus which our Father gladly gave us was an abundance of fruit. As we cleared the property we came across a bountiful array of fruit trees and fruit-bearing vines planted there years before. We had a veritable banquet of bananas, mangoes, passion-fruit, Surinam cherries and even the native mountain apples, Hawaii's only original palatable fruit.

All this abundant fruit augmented our diet, refreshed our bodies and enabled us to enjoy the results of our labor of love. It was as if it was the so-called "icing on the cake" of our adventure with God in this unpromising place.

At last came the day when our part in the project was completed. The property would now be taken over by those who would develop the site and lay out an elaborate building program. I told Lino, as best I could, that we would be leaving in a few days, moving on further down into the South Pacific.

The dear fellow's eyes filled with warm, shining tears. Taking my two calloused hands in his he looked longingly into my face and begged me to stay: "You no go!" he pled in anguish. "No go! You stay here! You live here. No go!"

But it had to be. Our Father had other work for us to do far, far away—far, far beyond our knowing.

Lino insisted on sending us off with a farewell banquet from his humble home. His whole family came. There were bowls and bowls of steaming shrimp, fried chicken, boiled pork, fried rice, baked beans and greens. He sat close to me and piled my plate until I could not eat another mouthful.

At dawn the next day we left for New Zealand. Lino was there to bid us farewell. All of us wept openly without shame. Our Father had given us not only the strength and stamina to meet a challenge, but also love, loyalty and laughter to brighten our days. *Thank You, Father.*

Chapter 2

New Zealand Lessons

From my earliest childhood the paths of my life had intersected those of New Zealanders. Some had been sturdy pioneer families on the frontier of early life in Kenya. Others had been the fine young men who came to Canada for pilot training during the Second World War. Wherever I met them their cheerful good will, their integrity, their fine and courteous conduct impressed me deeply.

These New Zealanders always displayed enormous loyalty to their rugged, ocean-battered homeland, deep down in the South Pacific. They spoke glowingly of its snow-sheathed Southern Alps; of the rolling rangelands grazed by millions of sheep and cattle; of the rich farms adorned by neat homes; of rugged pristine beaches lying beautiful beneath the sun.

So late in life, in my early fifties, a strong insistent compulsion gripped me to go there to start a new adventure in living. Spurred on by the enthusiasm and vision of our pastor in Hawaii, it seemed certain we could find some spot in which we could serve God's purposes for His people in the South Pacific.

Already I had friends who had gone to the South Pacific as Christian workers. One couple was in Fiji. Another was working with Cook Islanders who had immigrated to New Zealand. On our way, we spent time with both families who showed us firsthand how urgent was the need for a renewed Christian outreach in the region.

What I had neglected to do was to ascertain, beyond any question, whether or not New Zealand was in fact the place where my Father wanted us to serve Him.

I say this in sincerity, for at the time, circumstances—and the encouragement of our associates—certainly led us to believe that New Zealand was the place for us. Time was to prove otherwise. There would be months and months during which nothing opened up for us to do except to wait upon our Father's time and direction.

This is no easy experience for any of us who truly wish to follow Christ. Too often our keen enthusiasm takes us into appealing paths which, though they seem legitimate, are not necessarily those of His choice. It is at such times we marvel at His patience (and perseverance) with us. We look back in retrospect and give humble thanks for our Father's loving hand upon us. We are quietly astonished that He is so gracious and generous in drawing us back into His own paths and purposes for our little lives.

It has always been an enormous consolation to me to realize that my Father alone fully understands the deep longings of my spirit. Over and over I have poured out my profound appreciation to Him for His capacity to fathom the inner yearning of my soul that I might love Him more fully and serve Him more devotedly. And, if, at times, in eagerness and the excitement to do His bidding, we somehow miss the turn in the path, He is ever there to draw us back gently and set our feet again surely on the way of His choosing.

This was to happen in New Zealand. It was to be one of the most powerful lessons, one of the most profound principles I was to learn in my spiritual pilgrimage. For, though outwardly Ursula and I found ourselves amongst the most gracious people in some of the most magnificent scenery on earth, we were not precisely in the place of His choice. This did not diminish our delight in exploring the Islands. It meant, however, there was no definite, dynamic direction to our days.

I had shipped our little truck and camper from Hawaii to New Zealand. It must have been one of the first such outfits ever to be seen in the country twenty years ago. People would follow us for miles and miles. Then, when we parked, they would pull up behind us to ask quietly if they could just peek inside. They were all so intrigued by our little "home on wheels." We often remarked in fun that if we had charged an admission fee of $1.00 a visitor, it would easily have paid our fuel costs from week to week. Some of those who came in asked for permission to draw up floor plans so they could go home and build similar units for themselves.

At the time there were very rigid regulations restricting the importation of motor vehicles. So on the roads we encountered an astonishing array of vintage cars and trucks, most of them maintained by the remarkable skill and ingenuity of their owners or expert mechanics. Many of the replacement parts had to be built by local people in their own humble machine shops. This was a tremendous tribute to their determination to keep their vehicles in service.

We were to be recipients of their skilled services. From time to time, for one reason or another, our truck simply would not start. I would have to trudge up a remote country road to find a farmer or local mechanic who could help us. It never ceased to astonish me how quickly, eagerly, happily, total strangers would come to our aid.

In short order they would determine the difficulty, put things right, and have us on the road again. Not once did any of them charge for their time or expertise. Though we offered to pay, they refused to be reimbursed. Instead, they waved us away with a warm handshake and broad smile.

This was the second great lesson learned in New Zealand. The common people were so ready to help others in trouble. Finding such deep delight in lending a helping hand, they had neither the desire nor the inclination to charge for their assistance to strangers. They really did love others as they loved themselves. Making money simply was not the main motive in life for them. Being of benefit was!

We encountered this amazing, lovely attitude again and again all over both the North and South Islands. It was not something restricted to rural people who were glad to share themselves with strangers. We found this gracious, generous, great-hearted spirit even in real estate agents who insisted on entertaining us in their homes. We came across it in a young attorney who took the time to introduce us to all the local officials in his town who could possibly help us locate a suitable home. Not a cent would he take for his time and advice, even though he put himself at our service for most of an afternoon.

Here were professional people who, in the midst of their careers, felt constrained to lay down their lives, their time, their skills at our disposal without any ulterior motive of personal gain or advantage. It touched me deeply. In vivid, living colors it made me see how our Father really wanted us to care for one another unconditionally. And the surprising thing was that these ordinary—yet very extraordinary—people, made no special claim to be pious or religious.

The private impact made upon my personal life was enormous. Not only did I learn a dynamic lesson in how to live a fully joyous life, but I was also reminded again of my Father's enduring faithfulness in caring for us with such tenderness, generosity and love in a faraway place amongst complete strangers.

Again and again I would bow my spirit in utter humility and unbounded gratitude for the wondrous way in which He supported us through total strangers. The more we explored the Islands month after month, moving gently along all the winding roads that criss-crossed the mountains and valleys, the more we were enamored of this lovely land. Its shining mountains, its singing streams, its exquisite beaches, its fertile farms, its gentle climate, its gracious people were all that anyone could wish.

Yet, somehow, in a strange but supernatural manner, the impression came ever more clearly to me that this was not where our work was to be. There was a gentle, ever-increasing inner conviction that New Zealand was but a stepping stone, as it were, across the Pacific to some other place of service perhaps much less appealing.

Sometimes in the solitude of a flaming sunset on a deserted beach, or in the stillness of a sunrise over a soaring mountain range, I would pour out the longing of my soul to my Father, entreating Him to make His way clear. If indeed my footsteps had gone astray on this far strand of land, I was prepared to turn back and take the trail, any trail, He chose for me.

In all of this Ursula gave her unstinting love and loyalty. She did not attempt to force any issue or assert her own personal wishes. In her own genial way she was prepared to accept whatever choices I felt constrained by God's Spirit to make. If we were to stay in New Zealand, we would stay. If we were to move on, then we would move on. It was just that simple! Like two small, tender-hearted children, we quietly entrusted ourselves to our Father's care. It was the waiting that was hard!

While we waited we were not idle. Hidden coves, secluded beaches and exciting new mountain ranges invited us to explore. There were quiet trails to follow, exotic species of birds and wild animals to discover. Everywhere we went our spirits were awed and stilled by the magnificent seascapes and landscapes of these lovely Islands. And along the way we made friends with the local people who took us into their homes and into their hearts.

It was during this interlude that there began to take form in my mind a book that would deal with handling stress in life from a purely Christian perspective. Never before had the ideas and outline for a book come to me so clearly. It would be called *Taming Tension.* Little did I dream then how difficult it would be to get it published. Yet eventually it would be used by God all around the world to touch, inspire, enlighten and uplift thousands of men and women who read it.

Ursula, too, found special pleasure in projects suited to her skills. One of these was knitting. We had gone in search of the finest wool available in this land of many sheep. With flying fingers she made me a magnificent sweater that would shelter me from the sharp, damp winds that blew in off the southern oceans. I loved to wear it on my long hikes in the hills.

It had one enormous drawback. Whenever the weather was damp outdoors the sweater would simply S-T-R-E-T-C-H and S-T-R-E-T-C-H and S-T-R-E-T-C-H—until it resembled a bulky blanket draped about my body! With daring courage Ursula undid the whole garment. She then rewound the wool and proceeded to crochet another cardigan for me. It, too, S-T-R-E-T-C-H-E-D. So we laughed and laughed and finally gave the garment to a friend who wrapped it around himself when he milked his cows on frosty mornings.

One day a dear family who owned a beautiful sheep ranch, noticing how much I suffered when the weather turned cool and damp, prevailed upon me to go and see a country doctor in a nearby village. The dear fellow was so busy, and his practice so crowded, his receptionist said he could not take me for several days. He was in a back room, examining a patient, and overheard her remarks. At once he came out and invited me to come up to his home during lunch.

Sitting comfortably on the couch in his living room, he asked me quietly what the difficulty was. I replied that I had suffered much as a young man from arthritis in my spine and hips. Gently he proceeded to tell me I had come to the worst possible place for this affliction. Because of New Zealand's topography (it is a small land mass in the path of the chill winds of the southern oceans) and its dampness and coolness, I was bound to have complications. With great regret he urged me to leave at once. He spent his entire noon hour chatting with me. When we parted I offered to pay him. He laughed heartily. "My dear man," he exclaimed, "I have done nothing for you, except to keep you out of trouble!"

It was a typically generous New Zealand gesture of good will!

But where to go? What to do?

A few days later our Father answered those searching questions for us. In the post came a little blue air mail message from Australia. A young man whom I had met at a summer camp in Canada, years before, begged us to come over and help establish a camp for university people in Australia. At last the waiting was over. Our Father had opened the door to a new chapter in life. We were ready and eager to go.

Chapter 3

Australian Action

When our camper was unloaded on the docks at Sydney, the authorities immediately advised us that it could not be used in Australia unless the vehicle was changed from left-hand drive to right. This change would be very costly and complex. They gave us one other option, however. We could take it all the way down to Canberra, the nation's Capital Territory.

This meant our headquarters would have to be made somewhere in that general area. It was hundreds of miles from Sydney where our friends were located. At first appearance it seemed an impossible situation. But our Father had special purposes in mind for taking us all the way down to the foothills of the Snowy Mountains, Australia's loftiest range.

Winter was approaching as we explored the Capital Territory. The dawn would break with the whole country encrusted in thick white frost. Inside our cramped little camper it was chill as an icebox. Our steaming breath would condense on the cold windows and there freeze into sheets of translucent ice and frost. It was hardly the usual setting one pictured of the scorching "outback."

It soon became clear to us that for the most severe winter months we would have to seek the shelter of a warmer climate at the coast. But before we did, the entire countryside around Canberra had been carefully combed for a possible site to start a camp for university people.

Our friends came all the way down from Sydney to see what we had found. Huddled together in the close quarters of the camper we prayed earnestly for wisdom and direction in establishing this new enterprise. We came to the daring conclusion that if such a project was in our Father's best purposes, He could provide the place. Carefully we drew up a prepared statement as to what our objectives were. I then suggested it be submitted to the Commonwealth (Federal) government, in the hope they might see fit to provide some assistance. It was a bold act of faith which I felt confident God would honor in His own unique way.

Ursula and I then left for the coast. We were drawn to a secluded little seaside village in a lovely location called Tuross Head. It was remarkable rolling country with large lakes, surrounded by native forest adjacent to the sea. There were miles of open sand beaches where the southern seas thundered on the shore in giant breakers driven by the winter weather.

Here we rented a bright cottage overlooking the coast and I set to work at once writing *Taming Tension*. It was a useful way to fill in the time while we waited to see what response the government would make to our bold overtures. We gradually built bonds of friendship with some of our neighbors. One pioneer family invited us to occupy their great rustic house while they went away on an extended holiday.

Here, high on a hill, with breath-taking views in every direction, we settled into the austere setting of an ancient estate that resembled an old English feudal castle. It was hardly like home. But we made the best of its huge rooms, rambling verandahs and rugged sheet iron roof.

Then one night a message came. Our friends from Sydney were very excited. The government had offered them a 100-acre site. We must come and see it!

A couple of days later we met at the spot. It was one of the most bleak and barren chunks of desolate wasteland I had ever set foot upon. Only one small, stunted, wind-battered Eucalyptus tree grew on a wretched rock out-crop. The whole scene made my blood boil. At best the offer was a bad joke. I told my associates they would simply have to go back to the authorities and refuse their wretched offer. Surely the Commonwealth government could come up with a much better site than these derelict acres.

My younger friends were uneasy about this. So we sat in the shade of the single, scrubby tree and prayed for courage and fortitude to face the authorities again. I was sure our confidence in Christ would be honored.

Again there was a long silence of several weeks. Then once more the news came to the big old house. Our friends were utterly ecstatic. They had been given a lovely block of 600 acres, lying secluded in the rolling foothills of the Snowy Mountains. The property was all in paddocks, bisected by a beautiful trout stream. It was a frontier sheep station and would be perfect for the purpose in mind. My spirit leaped with sheer joy! I exulted in gratitude for the great faithfulness of our Father God.

The way was opening up for stirring dreams to come alive. I was thrilled with this new turn of events. As we went up to look over the land I sensed it was in truth a unique spot of special attractiveness and unusual potential. As with the camp in Hawaii, it was in rough shape. Lying at the very end of a road deeply rutted, ruined by winter floods, it was cut off in heavy weather because of the racing mountain stream that had never been bridged. It had to be forded.

Still, in spite of the isolation, Ursula and I offered to go and pioneer the place. Little did we know what we faced.

Only a few days later I awoke in the middle of the night with excruciating pains in my chest and upper torso. It was as if I had been placed in an enormous steel vise and pressure was being applied to crush my whole rib cage. Stabbing pains raced into my shoulders and upper arms. Some spasms were so severe they virtually took my breath away. My head and neck throbbed and pounded with agony. Perspiration oozed from every pore until I was drenched. In torment I turned and twisted, struggling to grasp another breath, longing for a moment's respite.

It seemed certain I would die, though actually death held no great dread for me. In fact, in the intensity of my suffering it would have come as a welcome release. Ursula and I spoke of this in subdued tones. She showed sterling courage in the midst of our crisis. Gently she applied cool damp cloths to my brow. Quietly she massaged my chest as the pains raged through my body hour after hour.

The great old house where we stayed had no telephone. The nearest neighbors were more than a mile away at the bottom of the hill in the utter darkness. Ursula did not drive, and it was impossible for me even to raise my head from the sweat-stained pillow. So we were utterly alone, yet not alone in our ordeal. Our Father was there.

In her quiet confidence in Him Ursula said softly, "Darling, you will not die!" A gentle smile enfolded her face: "Our Father still has much work for you to do in this world."

So together, in mutual support, we waited for the dawn to break. With the first daylight she would walk across the fields to find help from a neighbor.

The couple to whom she went through the dew-drenched grass were sturdy pioneers of the outback. His father had been a frontier country doctor who rode his horse all across the bushland to tend his patients. Without a moment's delay he made up his vehicle into a makeshift ambulance, threw a few home remedies into a bag and raced up to the house. He was determined to haul me into the nearest hospital, twenty-seven miles away, along a twisting, rough country road.

By the time he came, however, I was too weak to move, too spent with suffering even to lift my head. I was too wrung out with agony and sweat to have an ounce of strength left ever to reach the hospital. Besides, I had very little confidence whatever in doctors. So I decided, live or die, I would face the consequences in the surroundings of my own home on the hill. I did agree to swallow some of the pills the dear fellow brought in his bag. I was sure they could not possibly increase my pain, and they might just ease the ache in my bursting skull.

For days and days I did nothing but lie supine on my back. My strength was spent. No energy remained! I lay almost as inert as a log. The doctor in the distant town had been told of my condition and insisted I be brought in. Just as adamantly I refused to be moved. So, for more than a week, I lay there, ministered to gently by Ursula, and Shelly, a beautiful big Golden Labrador Retriever who would come in to sit by the bed and lick my hands.

In about ten days enough energy began to course through my body that I could lift my head. A small surge of vitality encouraged me to believe recovery was remotely possible. Perhaps there could be another chapter left to my life. Hope for renewed health sprang up anew. If there was any faith at all for the future, it was found only in my Father and His care for me.

Suddenly one morning Ursula burst into my room. With bated breath and in urgent whispers she alerted me, "Honey, Honey! The doctor is here; the doctor is here!"

Since we love to tease each other, I was sure she was simply playing a little game to cheer me up. Before I was able even to collect my wits, a young woman came striding into the room a few steps behind Ursula.

This stranger's sudden appearance startled me. She was an attractive young person, attired in a brief mini-skirt, with high leather boots reaching almost to her knees. Jauntily she swung a black briefcase in one hand and a stethoscope in the other. I burst out laughing. It must be a mistake—a joke!

Striding up beside my bed without any formal introduction or professional niceties, she looked down into my face and growled angrily, "What's the matter with you anyway? Why didn't you come in to the hospital?"

Her accent was a dead giveaway. She was obviously not an Australian, but a Canadian. We soon learned that for a few weeks she was filling in for the resident physician away on holidays. When she discovered I was a Canadian, her belligerence softened. At least we both spoke the same dialect.

It turned out she was one of those daring young ladies bent on adventure. An honors graduate of McGill University in Montreal, she had spent her first practice among the Eskimos in the high Arctic. From there she had gone to serve among the Aborigines in Western Australia. Now she was passing through, enroute to a jungle tribe at the headwaters of the Amazon River in South America.

We were soon on common ground and got on well.

I assured her that I would indeed show up at the hospital when I had energy enough to drive the rough road to town. Eventually this did happen. All the tests that could be taken in that tiny, two-horse town failed to show what might be the trouble. To this day I have never bothered to find out. Sufficient to say that for the next two years it seemed I was only half a man. My level of energy was minimal. Every heavy piece of work was like a double load. I tired easily. Only my will and ironlike discipline of myself drove me on to find new strength from above.

This incident did not deter Ursula and me from our determination to carry out the pioneer work at the camp. I would not be capable of as much physical labor as before, but I could still bring to the project all the skills and extensive expertise in land management and livestock production that had been such a large part of my life up until then.

Finally one fine spring day we packed up our few personal belongings, loaded the camper for the road and headed for the foothills of the Snowy Mountains. Dear old Shelly came with us. She had been adopted into our tiny family and quickly took possession of us as though we in turn were her adopted children.

She was a magnificent big dog of golden color. The three of us could barely squeeze into the cramped front seat of our little camper. To the absolute consternation of Australians who passed or overtook us on the road, they would stare in utter disbelief at this huge dog apparently "driving" this awkward vehicle, for she sat on the right side where a driver "down-under" normally did. More than once they nearly drove us into the ditch as they tried to sort out the puzzle.

For us it was all a bit of fun and great high humor.

Chapter 4

Kangaroos, Cockatoos and Poisonous Pests

It has long been my deep conviction that one of our Father's most loving gifts to His earth children is laughter. Our capacity to see humor, even in tough places, can carry us over formidable frontiers. Our ability to find some fun, even in the darkest days, is a unique gift from God for which I have thanked Him sincerely all my life. Not only does this element of gaiety bring great good cheer into life's adventures with Him, but it also contributes gentle healing to our bodies and minds. It mends strained emotions; it uplifts sad spirits.

We needed a double dose of high humor to tackle the tough task of restoring the lonely sheep station that stood so forlorn at the very end of the winding country road. In fact, after the road crossed the last river ford and climbed the steep bank beyond, it degenerated into little more than a deeply rutted, rockstrewn sheep track. Only with the greatest caution and expert driving was it possible to drive the camper down the long trail to the rough frontier homestead.

To compensate for all this we were thrilled to find ourselves surrounded by an unusual array of Australian wildlife. Flights of brilliant Roselas flew through the parklike groves of Eucalyptus trees scattered across the paddocks. Lovely snow white Cockatoos were abundant. Sometimes a score would swoop along a fence, each in turn alighting on a fencepost, looking like a carved ornament in marble. Kangaroos grazed in the open pastures. The magnificent "Blue Flyers," gray Kangaroos, could sail across the rugged terrain, fallen trees and rough rocks with incredible ease and agility.

Even though my physical strength was at such a low level Ursula and I would spend several hours each day working on the road. There were deep potholes to fill with earth, rocks to roll away, run-off ditches to be dug and rough spots to be shoveled and raked smooth. Though it was old fashioned pick-and-shovel labor, it was not beneath our dignity to get in and do it with a will. We could see beyond the sweat and toil and aching muscles to the time when hundreds of people would drive down this road to find spiritual renewal for their jaded spirits in this spot.

Once the homestead was accessible we applied for a telephone to be installed in the house. Ursula was firmly determined that we should at least have this tenuous contact with the outside world "beyond the bush." She did not want us to be cut off from civilization again. It was well that she did, for we would need this phone line much sooner than ever expected.

Once the road was passable we set to work on the house. With her energetic thoroughness Ursula scrubbed and cleaned and polished the place. We were puzzled by holes that went right through the walls from one room to another. One day we would find out the startling story behind them. But not for a while!

Outside I did what I could to tidy up the yard and make the property a bit more presentable. I tore out old broken fences and picked up the sort of scraps and junk that often accumulate around frontier farms. I cleared away the broken down limbs of trees and brush growing about the place. It was all a labor of love. Little by little, day after blistering day, the place became steadily more attractive and parklike. There was a deep sense of solid achievement in our work. Also, it would bring pleasure to others.

The greatest adversity we ran into was the astonishing array of poisonous pests that flourished in this rough "out-back." Though I had spent over twenty years of my life in Africa, and felt rather inured to snakes, scorpions and hordes of insects, I was taken aback by the Australian bush.

First and foremost were the swarms of tenacious flies that made life a misery. Ursula attached long strings to the brim of my broad-rimmed bush hat. As they dangled down and swung around my face, neck and throat they would discourage the pests from creeping into my mouth, eyes and nostrils. Still I loathed them!

In the grass there were colonies of ants which equalled anything the "army ants" of Africa could ever do. Their bite was exceedingly painful and left the feeling that one had been set on fire. No wonder in some places they are referred to as "fire ants."

It startled me to discover so many venomous snakes in the rock outcrops and brush piles that littered the landscape. I had purchased a book that served as a guide to the reptiles and insects in our area. It was not reassuring. Quickly I learned to tread very carefully wherever I went in my work and to carry a stout stick for self-protection.

The great, horned lizards, bees, wasps and the huge array of other winged pests surprised me no end. Their variety and numbers almost equalled the wide array of Eucalyptus trees that grew at random all around us. Of these, some had poisonous pollen about which I knew nothing at all just then.

That is, until Christmas morning. At break of day, when I stirred from sleep, it was to find that I could not open my eyes. Both were swollen shut. I was totally blind!

In all my years of experiencing pain and suffering with various sorts of tropical diseases I had never encountered such intense agony. Unknown to me, the very virulent pollen from a Eucalyptus in the yard had been blown into my eyes as I mowed the dry grass beneath it. The poison in the pollen was so potent it ulcerated both eyeballs. Even to move an eye was to have the sensation it was filled with fragments of sharp, shattered glass that lacerated it within. So there I was, flat on my back—totally blind, unable to move, groaning with agony.

Ursula did not yet drive. So for a second time we were cut off from our neighbors. But there was the phone. In typical old-fashioned ways she still had to call out through a local country switchboard operator. The dear, dear lady detected that we were in deep trouble when Ursula asked for the hospital more than forty miles away. Immediately the operator asked if there was some help they could give us. When told what our dilemma was she said her husband would drive over at once and take me all the way in to the hospital—even if it was Christmas morning.

That trip of utter compassion and mercy from total strangers was an awful nightmare of suffering. Every jolt in the road, every rough spot, every turn of my head was absolute agony. A doctor had been alerted I was coming into emergency. His blunt statement was, "You have been working in the bush!" This affliction was considered one of the most painful ever suffered by human beings, he told me. Then he proceeded to freeze my eyes, provided me with a special salve, and sent me home.

The treatment seemed to be only a temporary benefit. The blindness persisted and so did the pain. Then Ursula recalled how in her childhood Camomile—Flower—Tea had been used for injured eyes. What a relief!

Day after dismal day we brewed the tea, and when it cooled, splashed the dark liquid into my burning eyes. Its healing benefit was like a balm. I had asked my Father, in childlike confidence, to use any means He chose to restore my sight. Again and again Christ had brought healing to the blind in His day. His touch had not changed across the centuries. He could do the same for me!

But the road back to recovery seemed painfully slow. For weeks I could barely make out the shapes of large objects such as trees or buildings. Smaller objects were blurred and indistinct. The capacity to focus my vision at all seemed lost entirely.

Since my brush with death at the early age of thirty-five when doctors gave me up as destined to die within six months, I had very little confidence in the medical profession. So I seldom sought any sort of medical aid except in extreme emergencies.

After long waiting for my eyes to focus, I decided to phone an eye specialist in Canberra. He was highly agitated by what I told him. He insisted I be brought in early the next morning. My rather simple but startling reply was that I would come only if it was in accord with my Father's will and wish for me.

Unsure of exactly what should be done at dawn, we retired early. About midnight I was awakened by a tremendous cloudburst of rain pounding on the sheet iron roof. Only those who have lived in Australia can grasp the full impact of the ferocious downpours typical of that region. Hour after hour the rain spilled out of the dark clouds. When the dawn finally broke, gray and dull and overcast, I knew we were cut off from Canberra. Torrents of muddy water rampaged down the streams we could no longer ford.

We phoned the specialist, explaining our predicament. He insisted again that I come in just as soon as the flood waters subsided, perhaps in a day or two.

That afternoon, taking a stick in hand to support my steps more surely, I decided to take a brief walk across the paddocks to try and ascertain what damage the storm had done. Suddenly, out in the middle of one of the grassy meadows, I noticed a startling change in the scenery around me. Rocks, fenceposts, shrubs—all began to come into clear view. My capacity to focus my vision sharpened and intensified. It was as if a dim gray veil was being removed from my vision by an invisible hand.

I returned to the ranch house ecstatic to share the joy and pleasure with Ursula. All I could shout was "Thank You, Father! Thank You, Father!"

I never went in to see the eye specialist. Nor have I ever been to see an oculist. When these lines are read I will be seventy years of age. I do not wear glasses, even though I spend an enormous amount of time in reading and study. To this day I have remarkable sight and revel joyously in the beauty of the world all about me. My Father restored my vision!

With renewed vigor I applied my scientific skills in land management to the development of a master plan for the 600 acres entrusted to us. The application of rotational grazing for livestock, the development of permanent pastures, the strategic employment of local water supplies, the possible use of irrigation, the location of buildings, roads and service areas were all laid out with care.

Soon two younger men and their families would move out to the station. It would be their responsibility not only to implement the master plan prepared for them but also to initiate the work with people whom God brought to them.

These latter would be university staff and students drawn to our center from larger cities. Part of our simple strategy for the camp was that anyone who came had to make some sort of tangible contribution to the project. Both men and ladies were expected to donate some of their time, energy and strength to do the work that needed to be done.

This led to some interesting and amusing events. One professor of psychology was put to work with pick and shovel to dig deep pits for our first outdoor privies. At the end of his first day of hard labor he climbed out of the hole covered in dust and dirt, but his face was wreathed in smiles. His terse comment was, "That is the first day in my life I could look back and actually see the work I accomplished. And it is wonderful, wonderful!"

Another brilliant architect was asked to build a large chicken house. He produced the most elaborate plans that were ever devised for such a simple structure. As he built it, every piece was fitted with meticulous precision. Little did those laying hens realize what prestigious quarters they occupied when his professional job was done.

Week by week our work went on. Little by little my strength increased so that I could at least carry on the responsibilities entrusted to me. From my personal perspective it was a token of my Father's gracious care that though I had been so very, very ill, He supplied the strength and energy needed to do the work that came to hand.

As we tidied up the homestead, repaired fences, eradicated weeds and cleared away the old debris, the whole place became pleasing to the eyes, a solace to the soul, an uplift to the spirit. Here men and women would come to meet the Master in personal encounters of eternal duration.

Chapter 5

The Holes in the Walls

The rancher and his wife who had pioneered this sheep station came back to visit it from time to time. They seemed intensely interested in our work there and over the course of that first year became dear friends. They showed us special kindness as newcomers to the country, sharing their own special frontier skills with us, often bringing us gifts of fresh produce from their new farm.

One day they decided to tell us the astonishing story of how the holes in the walls were made. It is recounted here as clearly as I can recall it for two special reasons. The first is to convey to the reader the rough, tough frontier setting in which we were located. Secondly, it shows how our Father can take the most unlikely places and most unlikely people to achieve His own winsome work in the world. For in due time not only was this ranch to become a special place for His people, but also this dear couple would come gently into His family.

So here is the heart-stopping story:

Just at dusk one evening a dilapidated old truck approached the ranch house in a cloud of red dust. A rough, grizzled character climbed out of the vehicle after parking it right in front of the humble home. The rancher went out to meet the stranger who said he was a trapper. He requested permission to trap foxes on the land rising around the ranch. Not keen to have strangers on his property, the rancher replied he would first go in the house to discuss it with his wife.

As he turned to do so the trapper pushed a smoke-blackened "billy can" into his hands. He asked him to fill it with boiling water so he could make his evening meal. It was an odd request and aroused the rancher's suspicion.

As they boiled the water the two discussed the stranger outside. "I think you should go out with your gun!" his wife insisted. So the rancher slipped a small revolver into his pocket and took the billy can of boiling water to the door.

He was met there by the stranger with a loaded weapon in his hands. In gruff tones he ordered the man back into the house, waved his weapon menacingly and ordered the wife to get a rope and tie her husband's hands behind his back. He was then forced to go and sit in a corner tied to a chair.

The grim gunman then demanded a pad of writing paper, a pencil and a hot cup of coffee. Seating himself at the crude little kitchen table, his rifle across his knees, he stated bluntly in angry tones: "I'm going to sit here and write out my whole life's confession. Then I'll take care of you two people." He was unaware that their two little girls had been put to bed early and were asleep in their tiny beds in the adjoining room.

Hour after hour the tough terrorist scribbled out his life story on the plain sheets of paper. Hour after hour the canny rancher's wife plied him with cups of coffee and whatever smooth patter she could muster in her hardy mind. She was not one to crack under stress or melt into tears in soft emotion. The chips were down and she was "playing for keeps."

Out of the corner of her eye she had watched her good man struggle surreptitiously with the rope that bound his hands. She had knotted the rope with frontier skill in such a way that she knew he could work his arms loose. Now she saw that he was almost free.

The trapper filled page after page of the pad, deeply immersed in recounting the awful escapades of his cruel life. It was a long and tragic litany of robberies, rape, murder and mayhem, a career of crime seldom matched in the country's violent outback. As later events showed, he was, in fact, Australia's most wanted criminal with a huge bounty on his head.

When his forlorn confession was completed he rose to his feet and started toward the brave frontier lady with menacing eyes. "I'll take care of you first!" he growled. "Then I'll take care of your man and then myself!"

At this she shouted to her husband, "Give him what you've got!" The rancher, his hands free now, whipped out his revolver and began to blast away at the intruder. A vicious gun battle broke out with bullets plowing holes through the thin walls, barely missing the wee girls in the room beyond.

In the melée there were close misses until finally a fortunate shot struck the trapper in the throat. The bullet gouged through the soft flesh, knocking him to the floor. Blood gushed out from the gaping wound. It looked as though he would surely die. The rancher, a rather gentle, quiet man, seemed stunned by the sudden turn of events. What to do now?

"I'll rush over to the neighbors for help!" his wife ejaculated. "You stay here—don't faint—and stand guard over this scoundrel!" They had no telephone and the only possible help would be to reach the closest ranch about a mile away across the roaring creek. With only a rough coat thrown over her night attire she set out through the darkness. There were fences to cross, paddocks to traverse, a fallen tree to find where she could scramble across the swollen stream.

By the time she beat on the neighbor's door with her bare hands she stood in tatters, her clothes torn to shreds from the wire fences, tree branches and brush through which she had scrambled. When the neighbors opened the door they could scarcely believe what they saw, much less the wild things she said. They were sure she had gone "Bushie"—an Australian term for those who become deranged by their lonely life in the bush.

Finally she prevailed on them to call the Canberra police. The response was immediate. By the time she and her neighbors could collect themselves, make the long round-about journey downstream and circle back to the remote ranch, the troopers were already there and had ringed the house with patrol vehicles.

The so-called trapper had not died, though he was close to the end from a massive loss of blood that reddened and stained the kitchen floor. Taken into custody, he was given immediate medical aid and hauled off to jail. There he made a full recovery, though in the end he chose to hang himself in his own cell.

But for our friends the story was not yet over. The weapon which the rancher used had not been properly registered in his name. And so, because of this minor misdemeanor, the law being rather ridiculous in some cases, charges for attempted murder were laid against the good man.

Happily, common sense finally prevailed in the courts after a lengthy drawn-out trial which very nearly undid the gentle sheepman. The odd and somewhat humorous irony of the whole ordeal was that eventually the crown acquitted the rancher but awarded the huge bounty to his wife. She straightway went out and bought a fine herd of cattle with her reward.

In a remarkable manner not a single member of the entire family had been injured in this incredible escapade. Still, the story made Ursula and me realize acutely how rugged and rough was this realm of the frontier where we had come to live and work for Christ.

Only a few days after being told this blood-tingling tale, we were just sitting down to our evening meal in this same kitchen. Looking out the window, I saw the same sort of ominous red dust cloud coming up the road. We were all alone. As the vehicle drew closer I could see it was a big black motorcycle mounted by a burly biker, attired in black leather leggings, black jacket and black beard. Like one of the notorious Hell's Angels, he came thundering into the yard with all the explosive power of his mount reverberating across the valley.

Like a stab of lightning thrust into our minds came the searing question which zig-zagged through our emotions: "Is this to be some sort of madcap replay of the dreadful drama enacted here by that awful trapper?"

In quietness, without uttering a word aloud, I lifted my spirit earnestly to my Father: "We are in Your care. Grant me Your wisdom and Your calm confidence in this crisis. Thank You, Father, for being here!"

I went to open the door. The biker all decked out in black already stood there, appearing very threatening indeed. He had dismounted swiftly and was at the point of pounding on the door.

"I'm from Sydney," he glowered. "Came here because I'd heard you have some sort of camp in these hills. Thought I'd spend some time here!"

His phrases came out short, sharp, in rapid succession like the staccato bursts from the tailpipe of his bike.

After plying him with a few pertinent questions, I invited him to come in and share our simple supper. Ursula was petrified, but to her great credit, did not show her apprehension. Quietly she set out a third place at the tiny table where this ominous stranger could eat with us—the same spot at which the wild trapper sat and wrote out his stunning confession of a lifetime of crime.

We were about halfway into the meal when the telephone jangled angrily on the kitchen wall. It startled all three of us. We were all a bit nervous, so I jumped, perhaps too quickly, from my chair to answer it.

It was the Canberra police on the line. Had I seen anything of a tough biker in our part of the backroads? He was wanted and a search was under way for his whereabouts. As calmly as possible, in full hearing of our unknown guest, I informed the police officer that in fact such a person had come into the ranch. What was more, the wanted man was at our table eating supper with us.

There was a strained silence on the line. Then the caller asked if we would mind if this formidable stranger spent the night with us. What could I say? I suppose it was okay—yet not okay! He then asked to speak directly to the biker who by now seemed to sense he was the object of our guarded conversation.

It turned out he was an offender, out on parole, who had failed to report his movements to the police. He was to spend the night with us, then report to the nearest police checkpoint next day.

Unsure of his behavior, we decided to let him sleep in the room with the bullet holes in the walls. Would it be a night of peace or one of mayhem?

Ursula and I elected to sleep outside in our camper. I chained our big golden Labrador to the back door. Then I dug out the old rusty hand axe from our tool chest and told Ursula to lay it by her bunk. I pulled out my razor sharp machete from Hawaii and placed it by my bed. It was like a grim replay of the nights I slept with a rifle by my bed all during our grim days of the Mau Mau terrorist threat in Kenya. At least we would not go down without a fierce fight.

Then, most importantly, we calmly entrusted ourselves to our Father's protection and waited for the night to pass. It did, in utter stillness! Dawn broke clear, bright and drenched with dew sparkling in the sun. Our guest had breakfast with us, then without fanfare roared off in a cloud of dust. We breathed easier and sighed softly, "Thank You, Father!"

Incidents of this sort were hardly calculated to insure a serene lifestyle in this spot. But it was all part and parcel of pioneer life for the sake of a cause much greater than our own interests. We were steadily laying the basic groundwork for those who would soon follow us in this place.

I still found that one of the most difficult adjustments was to encounter so many snakes. As a youth in Kenya, and then later when I returned to serve there as a scientist, I had more than my share of close calls with venomous Cobras, Puff Adders and Black Mambas. But here in this corner of the Australian bush I seemed to run into snakes at almost every turn, and they quite literally made my blood run cold, my hair to rise on end and my every muscle to become tense.

Sometimes I wondered how long we could handle this stress. Little did I know how suddenly and swiftly the entire direction of our future would change. In His mercy our Father had other plans and other places, of which I had never, ever dreamed, waiting for us to work and develop.

Chapter 6

South Pacific Days

We were delighted to see the two young men and their families move out onto the land. It was they who would bring to solid reality all the hopes and aspirations we held for the project. One of the stimulating aspects of advanced age is to see God's gracious Spirit stir and inspire those of the next and younger generation to great deeds for Christ's cause in the world.

It is akin to passing on the flame. In my own experience there had been older men and women who by their flaming faith in God had ignited my own small, flickering confidence in Christ. Our Father had proved Himself so utterly faithful to them. He would do likewise for me. So it was in turn my earnest hope that others younger than I would see the wonder of His care for me and so invest their utmost trust in The Most High.

From generation to generation our Father's work has been carried on in the world. This comes not just by the proclamation of His Word, vital as that is, but also by the simple, humble lives of men and women who trust Christ calmly for every aspect of life. It was the bright and radiant witness of a small company who truly walked with Christ in implicit faith who would convince others that our Father was in fact very active in their affairs.

In this connection between God and His children, one of the most convincing demonstrations of divine reality lies in the area of specific guidance and positive direction for those who are available to God's purposes. There is a sense in which one must be acutely sensitive to God's Spirit as counselor in our choices. It implies that one's will is subject to Christ's control. It means one is ready to move on short notice.

So it was that suddenly one day we were happily surprised to receive a brief letter from the pastor in Waikiki who had initially encouraged us to pioneer his camp on the Big Island of Hawaii. He was leading a tour all across the South Pacific, taking a group of Christian lay people to see the great need for renewed mission enterprises among some of the more remote islands. Eventually the tour would reach Sydney, Australia. He wanted so much to see us again. Would we meet him there?

With eager enthusiasm we drove the long miles to Sydney on the date of his arrival. Like family reuniting we flung ourselves into each other's arms. He had become like a father to us in loving concern. At lunch he began to unburden his soul. First of all, his splendid work in Waikiki was being threatened by an incursion of young charismatics who lacked solid teaching and clear understanding of God's Word. Would I consider coming back to begin regular Bible studies for his lay people?

Secondly, he had been presented with an unusual challenge in the New Hebrides. As was his custom, he had taken his tour group to visit one of the very large plantations that employed hundreds of local islanders. He had been given the honor to address the workers, speaking gently of the need for Christ in their lives. The response had been astonishing, not only in the number who responded but also in the conduct of their lives and labor.

The owner of the plantation was so impressed he wanted to reciprocate his appreciation in a tangible way.

So he offered the pastor 1,000 acres of raw jungle land. If he saw fit, perhaps he could use it to establish a training center there for the Island people. The question was, could such a scheme survive?

Knowing almost nothing about the challenges of developing viable enterprises in the tropics, the pastor asked if I would make the initial studies of the site. With my own firsthand experience in land management both in Canada and in Kenya, my skills would be of great value. Would I be willing to go to the New Hebrides and do a scientific survey for him?

The end result was that a couple of months later we boarded a plane which took us directly to the remote island capital. Arrangements had been made for us to stay in a pleasant guest house belonging to the plantation manager. A vehicle was put at our disposal and I was given letters of introduction to the leading government authorities on the island.

It was an intriguing interlude during which every possible effort was made to discover whether or not it was practical to start a training center. Across the centuries scores of mission enterprises in the tropics have foundered simply because they were not established on sound principles. Clearing dense jungle, husbanding fragile soils, finding suitable crops, combatting tropical pests and diseases involves a huge outlay of capital. And even then only the most skilled enterprises survive.

Spending days and days in the field, I spoke with those who were highly experienced in local land clearing. I visited the agricultural research station and spent hours in consultation with the men who had experimented with various crops to see if there might be some that would lend themselves to such an enterprise. The basic concept was that if a center were established it should be self-sustaining. There simply were no large sums of money available for launching this work.

Because of the extreme heat and humidity it was imperative to find some respite by swimming in the sea. Never before had I swum in such warm sea water. It was almost like taking a warm bath. Ursula just reveled in it. Nor had we ever seen such an abundant array of exquisite seashells. Some of the coves appeared to be still as primitive, unspoiled and untouched as any pristine place on earth. The blue waters, the shining sands, the lush green foliage, the awesome cumulus cloud formations combined to shape a tropical island paradise.

Yet, in stunning contrast, most of the islanders lived in appalling poverty. They had only grass or palm leaf huts with meager little gardens that could scarcely sustain their bodies. It seemed astonishing that in the late twentieth century so few of them were familiar with modern transportation. Standing at the edge of the rough country roads, they would watch us go by in amazed unbelief. Every black head would turn in wonder and follow our going with curious stares. Ursula found this hilarious in the extreme.

I was equally intrigued by the enormous land crabs that contested the island trails with us. They were huge, powerful creatures that could climb the palm trees and cut down the green coconuts. They fed on the rich, sweet flesh and milk of the developing nut. The result was that their own flesh was a delicacy.

The last night before our departure for Hawaii we were invited to a royal banquet at one of the plantations. What a feast of tropical dishes and exotic fruits. But by far the most delicious entree was the land crabs served with a fiery sauce resembling salsa.

Though our stay in the New Hebrides was rather brief, it left indelible memories that will always be cherished. Somewhat like Abraham's servant so long ago I felt sincerely: "I being in the way, the Lord led me . . . !"

Returning to Hawaii was, in a very deep sense, akin to coming home for us, even though we had no residence there. In their gracious and genial way, the pastor and his loving wife invited us to share their home until we could find modest accommodation for ourselves. This was a gracious gesture and a lovely reminder of our Father's gentle care for us. While searching for a little suite to stay in, we also spent the time preparing and typing up the full report of my studies in the New Hebrides. This was presented to the pastor for his final approval.

Finding accommodation at a price we could afford was not easy. For over two years the little camper had been our home on wheels. We had no rent to pay, no taxes to think about, no house to maintain. But now the camper was left behind in Australia, sold to an Aussie, and we were down to the bedrock of bare survival on what meager savings we had set aside. No one ever offered to pay us any sort of salary, so that wherever we served it was always freely without any hope or expectation of remuneration.

Our first small suite was not satisfactory. The adjoining units were occupied mostly by Samoans or other boisterous islanders who drank heavily and partied away much of the night. When I remonstrated with them their only response was to threaten to beat me to a pulp. So we moved to a second suite. Here there was more tranquility, but the rent was higher. It meant we could not even afford a second-hand car. If we went anywhere, we simply had to walk. Even our food, to some extent, would have to be foraged. I soon found mango and papaya trees growing on vacant lots that augmented our rather meager meals.

Still I saw this all as a new adventure in which our Father cared for us in loving and touching ways. The people we came to know in the community shared their garden produce with us. I stumbled across little food vendors who for a dollar or two would serve one a delicious heaping dish of curried chicken and rice. So it was fun to "make it" on a shoestring income in the heart of glamorous, gaudy, godless Waikiki.

The Bible studies which we started began to be well attended with people who longed for more than just the liturgy of the church. They came with a deep desire to truly know Christ and the living dynamic of His presence in their lives. Nor were they disappointed. Some of those classes were stirring sessions. The challenges of a cynical society were confronted with courage. There was a deep grounding in God's Word. And many were drawn into a close walk and precious personal communion with Christ.

Steadily, but surely, the de-stabilizing influences were put to route. Instead of preoccupation with highly charged emotional services, people began to long for a deep, serene walk with God. They discovered the great secret of studying His Word in sincerity and determining to do His will in quiet faith and implicit obedience. What a change!

Those were precious times shared in great earnestness with dear people drawn from all over the world. Honolulu and Waikiki were, in fact, a major mission field. Here millions of lost and weary souls came hoping to find an escape from the tyranny and tensions of a twisted society. The sun, the sand, the surf, the songs of the South Seas still could not assuage their inner yearning for the eternal life of the living Christ.

Often I would stand alone high on our balcony overlooking the bright lights and weep over Waikiki.

One very moving incident occurred at this time. It remains with me as a winsome reminder of how truly gracious our Father is to His children. Two earnest young couples came to the classes and became dear friends. The two men were twin brothers, born in the Puget

Sound area, sons of devout parents. Suddenly they were summoned home because of their father-in-law's unexpected death.

All his life the dear fellow had been an ardent salmon fisherman. He loved to take his little rowboat out on the Sound to catch the giant Chinook salmon. His ardent prayer had always been that he would die while out fishing.

One evening he did not come home at dark. So a search was launched. His wee boat was found way out on the Sound, moving slowly in great circles. When the searchers drew alongside they found the dear old gentleman slumped over dead in the tiny boat. At his feet lay a beautiful big fish. And on his line there was hooked another huge Chinook that was still towing the craft in slow circles. The sheer excitement of such an episode was the delightful call home from his Father.

It was a lovely incident and one I have treasured. My fond entreaty is that my Father may one day see fit to call me away from a mountain trail or brisk tramp along a surging shore. What a way to go!

Our return interlude in Hawaii was rather brief. The authorities had given us permission to stay only for a limited period, and that was at the pastor's special request. We had accomplished what we came to do. Now the moment to move on had arrived.

Much to our unbounded grief, this dear man of God was killed instantly in a head-on collision not long after. The whole Pacific region had lost a great man of broad vision.

Chapter 7

In Search of a Home

When we returned from overseas a dear friend who had recently lost his wife to cancer opened his home to us. It has always moved me deeply when people do this, for I see it as much more than mere human hospitality. Rather, it is the unique and lovely way in which my Father chooses to care for me as His child, through the gentle generosity of His people. I am always stirred in my spirit by such gestures of good will and cherish them as loving gifts from above.

Subsequently, another great-hearted family opened their home to us and helped us find another camper to replace the one we had used for nearly two years. A heartening little incident took place the day this unit was to be delivered to us. The driver who brought it down was an energetic, enthusiastic young fellow who had recently decided to devote his entire life to God's service as a missionary on the rugged west coast of Canada.

He was a total stranger to us. Still he seemed exceedingly keen to tell us the exciting story of his own stormy youth on the coast. Then he went on to recount how after he met Christ, some friends had given him a copy of *Splendor from the Sea*. This book which told of the exciting work of the Shantymen Missionaries on the West

Coast had finally convinced him to devote his whole life to the same sort of service.

Quietly we sat and listened to him recount all his experiences. Then, when at last he was done, I mentioned gently that he was in fact talking to the author of that book which God's gracious Spirit had used in his life. He was so startled, so astonished, so taken aback that for a few moments he could scarcely speak. What a coincidence we should meet!

Or was it? More than that, it was a moment of uplift for all of us.

Each of us in stillness and gratitude could only bow our heads and whisper softly, "Thank You, Father!"

It soon became apparent as winter approached with its rain, mist, fog and clinging dampness along the coast that we would have to move inland, up to the dry but cold mountain valleys. My ancient and persistent arthritic affliction could only be counteracted by the desert climate of the Okanagan region. I had found respite here twelve years before from the ravages of this dread disease. So I knew it was imperative to return again if I was to avoid being crippled up by it.

It seemed to us, as we sought specific guidance from our Father, that the time had come to procure a home. But this was not easy to do, given the human limitations I faced. The amount of savings which I had to purchase a home was quite meager. The real estate agents we approached simply shook their heads in despair, saying that there were no homes even listed at our price.

It should be explained here that I believed very simply that as God's child I was not to incur heavy debts by taking on a mortgage. Insisting that we should pay all cash in full for whatever we purchased, I refused to be bound into debt to anyone. Only in this manner could I be fully free to serve my Master wherever He might choose to call me or lead me.

Secondly, it should be pointed out that my funds for a home were rather meager simply because in the past what money I had made from ranching had been shared generously with others in need. I had not hoarded what had been earned in abundance. Rather, it had been given to God's service with an open hand in glad abandon. Nor was there ever reason to regret this action. In His turn our Father always provided for us—and He would do so again.

So it would be another adventure in quiet faith to seek and knock and find the place He had prepared for us. The autumn weather grew sharper, colder. Frost, white and menacing, began to sheath the camper at night. Winter was steadily settling down from the higher ranges, moving south menacingly from the arctic.

We roamed all the back roads, hoping to stumble on some simple little home someone might wish to sell at a lowly price. But there was nothing. One Sunday, camped high in the hills, we turned on our tiny radio and picked up the morning service from a local church down in the valley. The pastor had spoken only a few moments when I turned to Ursula and remarked, "That man truly knows Christ!" A broad grin creased my face: "If we settle in this area that is the church we will attend!" Little did we know the full import of that very simple statement.

The north winds blew stiffer. November had passed. December, with its long nights and short, cold days, had come—and still no home. Then one blustery night I picked up a local newspaper and scanned its property listings. There was one which appeared to be a distress sale, without an address, only a phone number. When I called from a pay phone my heart sank. The lady who replied could speak only in garbled tones. I was sure she was intoxicated. Still, I took the address and we agreed to meet at the home next morning.

I grunted to Ursula in dismay: "Don't expect too much. I'm sure it is an intoxicated woman on the bottle. It is probably just a pile of junk!"

Still, hoping against hope, we drove to the house next morning. To our astonishment it was a handsome house in a lovely location overlooking the lake.

My heart, still so weary from the Australian ordeal, began to hammer against my ribs. My pulse began to race erratically. Sweat broke out on my face and palms though it was so cold. Did I get the right address from the garbled conversation? Could this be the place?

Eventually, after some delay, a beat-up old ranch truck rattled around the corner and drove into the yard. The driver was a rough looking young rancher. From the other side of the cab stepped a lovely European lady, smiling warmly.

As soon as she began to speak I realized she not only had a pronounced foreign accent, but also a very serious speech impediment. She could hardly form words at all. Immediately she ushered us into the lovely home and began to pour out her story.

She and her husband were new immigrants from Europe. They had bought this house, assuming a modest mortgage. He had an excellent position as an engineer with a local mill. Then they found another home they liked even better. Again they bought it with a large mortgage. Just then the mill closed down; he lost his job; and now they were in a dire predicament. In desperation they had dropped the price to rock bottom. She begged us to buy it.

All previous efforts to sell had failed because of a serious mix-up over its proper registration. Her attorney had worked on the case for two years without success. I was not much interested in a home to which I could get no clear title.

Still in a simple act of faith I drew out my check book and wrote the lady a check for $500.00. "I am giving this to you in good faith. If clear title can be provided within a month we will pay your price." The price, by the way, was unbelievably low and exactly the amount we had set aside for a home.

The dear lady was so utterly overcome with gratitude she promptly held my arm and placed the keys to the house in the palm of my hand. "You move in today," she exclaimed happily. "It is your home!"

We tried to explain we only had the camper and not a single stick of furniture to our name. "Well, then, I will give you the kitchen set," she exclaimed happily. "And you can use the bed until you get your own!" Then, her face all wreathed in smiles, she drove off in the old truck.

Wonder of wonders, just ten days later her attorney informed us that suddenly, as by a miracle, the legal tangles had been unsnarled. He had worked for two years to resolve the impasse. We could proceed to purchase at the agreed price. And he delivered a clear title.

It was a subdued, joyous, humble couple who had found the precise property prepared so carefully for them by a caring, loving Father. Not only had we found a lovely home, but we had come into the place of Christ's special choice for us just then!

In that spot, bit by bit, week by week, my meager physical strength began to be rebuilt again. It would take nearly two full years to regain my former energy. As I dug a vegetable garden, mowed the lawns, trimmed the trees, hauled rocks to build up the rockeries and gradually improved the house, my muscles, tendons and bodily vigor responded in growing vitality. I was truly making a marvelous recovery and it was thrilling.

For more than two years I had not put pen to paper. Yet now again the old urge to write returned. We began to hold Bible studies in our home. And out of those sessions came truths that many asked me to put into a book. Seated in my office looking over the blue waters of Okanagan Lake I wrote *A Layman Looks at the Lord's*

Prayer. It would become another Christian classic read all over the world in many languages.

Our adventures in this home were continuous demonstrations to us of how gently our Father did care for us even in the smaller details of life. I had to make some minor alterations in the kitchen. This entailed removing some of the hanging cupboards. Not being an expert cabinet man, I simply took saw in hand and began to cut through the wall.

Something suddenly impressed upon me that I should stop in the midst of my sawing. I am completely confident it was the restraining influence of The Guardian Angel whom our Father provides for each of His children. For had I taken another stroke or two of the saw I would have cut through the main electrical cable bringing the high voltage line into the kitchen. It could easily have electrocuted me. I could calmly breathe again, "Thank You, Father!"

Because we had no furniture to begin with, Ursula and I brought the cushions and seat backs from the camper into the house. We scattered these around the spacious front room so that we could recline on them in the place of sitting on chairs or chesterfields. Some of our first guests later confided to us that they had the impression we had "gone modern." We laughed heartily over this.

Still it was true that when people began to pack into the house for weekly Bible studies, some did have to sit on the floor, or on the fireplace hearth, or even on the steps leading up to the other rooms.

This did not bother us a bit. In His loving way our Father sent people along with various pieces of exquisite furnishings. One dear fellow showed up with a handsome reclining rocker. I had never even sat in such a chair, much less owned one.

Another young lady offered us a collection of exquisite fine china cups and saucers from which we could serve refreshments after the services. Each of these were beautiful bonuses bestowed upon us in generous love from our Father's heart through the hands of His caring people. And for us it was a sweet and very precious reassurance of His personal provision for us.

All sorts of people from all types of backgrounds were drawn by Christ's gentle Spirit to these studies. They were never advertised publicly. No attempt was ever made to advertise the classes. It was simply a case of one person telling another about the life-changing truths that could be found in this simple home as we met with the Living Christ from week to week.

Professional people such as doctors, dentists and business executives were coming. But we also had rough cowboys, loggers, ranchers and laborers show up. Some came from homes where they had never known anything about God's Word. Others had been in the church most of their lives but knew only its empty forms and traditional liturgy. This now was their first encounter with The Living Christ. And just as in the days when He tramped the hot hills of Galilee, they were very excited and eager to meet and know Him.

When all is said and done Christianity is not the ornate structure of the church. It is not some complex body of belief. It is not the intellectual grasp of some spiritual doctrine. Christianity in essence is "knowing Christ." It is coming into such a simple and open encounter with Him that He does in truth transform all of life for us. We are no longer ever the same again. It is He who remakes us forever.

This we would see happen again and again in the house on the hill. It was by far the most wonderful aspect of our short stay in that lovely spot.

Chapter 8

The Old Violin

He came to our valley during the days when campus upheavals were common. He had been in the forefront of the fury that trampled on the flag, flung off all authority and challenged old traditions. His own life had been threatened amid the mayhem; so, to escape, he and his wife fled north to find refuge in our interior mountains.

The elderly educator was an individual of fine intellect and brilliant mind, but he had never truly met Christ. He knew nothing of the close and dynamic companionship of The Living God. His long academic career, his outstanding musical talents had somehow come to nothing but futility. His life had no ringing joyous resonance to it. Rather, it bore a sour note, filled with cynicism and bitterness.

He had heard that we were having Bible studies in our home. One day he called up and we invited him to come around for a little visit so we could become acquainted. He came alone the first night and spent several hours in our home.

Quietly we sat and listened to his long and bitter diatribe against all of life. Seldom had I met a man so set against society. A stream of contempt and scorn and sarcasm poured from his lips. His angry spirit burned hot against his family, his associates and his world. So much so, that by his own admission, he really had no friends and his days were filled with discord.

As he ranted on, the question which came to me over and over was: "How can I build a bridge of compassion to this dark and troubled soul? Oh, my Father, enable me to find common ground with him!" It was a simple prayer of profound concern for one so deep in distress.

Then he mentioned music. He told of his great love for the clarinet which he played with unusual skill, and he spoke of the fine orchestras in which he had played. He pointed out that one of his brothers was a professor of music at one of the great universities in the east.

It was the cue for which I had been waiting. Warmly I shared with him my own great interest in classical music. I recounted the days when I spent hours and hours practicing the violin. But that beautiful instrument had long since been donated to a school for the benefit of students who could not afford a good violin. So I asked the old gentleman to let me know if he ever stumbled across a lovely violin. At once a first strand of understanding was flung across the canyon of conflict that might have separated us.

He began to come to the classes, but his presence there created enormous controversy. One night in a burst of outrage he leaped to his feet. Grasping his brand new Bible in both hands, he flung it on the floor in black fury: "If that is supposed to be truth, I don't want any part of it!" he shouted angrily.

His behavior intimidated most of those attending the class. Ladies especially were terrified by his tirades. But I refused to back away from him. Firmly I insisted we were examining truth as God Himself revealed it to us in Christ Jesus. And he as a man could either choose to accept or reject that divine disclosure.

Several times I wrote him strong letters suggesting

that he should stay away. Not one was ever mailed. Always the Gracious Spirit of God constrained me to persevere with his perverseness. Still I wondered how long I would have to wait for some response from this twisted soul. His dear wife, a devout woman, had confided to me privately she was on the point of leaving him.

For some thirty-five years she had prayed for his conversion. Still his spirit seemed to become more sinister, his conduct more cruel, his behavior ever more belligerent. For her, life had become a hell. I begged her to remain steadfast in her faith that Christ could change this man. We made a quiet, mutual compact to trust our Father for a total transformation of this tough, abrasive character.

Then suddenly, early one Sunday morning, the phone rang. In his haughty, dictatorial way he insisted that I should come over to his home and watch TV with him. When I explained carefully that I had several services to conduct that day, and would be so exhausted it was unlikely I would be good company, he flew into a rage: *"I knew you didn't care about me!"* he roared, then crashed the phone down on the receiver.

I immediately called back. I told him I did indeed care and would be over very late in the day, after taking a brief rest.

When Ursula and I arrived at his home he was alone. The television was turned up full volume. In a casual gesture of utter condescension he waved us to a seat, then began to try and shout at me above the noise of the TV.

After a few minutes of this mayhem I stood up and spoke firmly: "Either we sit quietly and watch the program or we shut it off and have a chat!"

He was furious! Jumping to his feet he strode over to the set, slammed it shut, then in a rage glared at me in angry defiance. "All right, Keller, give it to me! What do you have to say?"

Without flinching I looked him full in the face and replied: "I will give it to you! I have a message from The Most High just for you! Sit down!"

To my astonishment he complied at once and more or less collapsed onto the couch beside me. Briefly, boldly, I pointed out that his intense academic arrogance, his overpowering intellectual pride, his cynical belligerence against both man and God had in fact kept Christ out of his life. Though the Savior had come to him again and again, seeking admission to his life, he had deliberately and willfully slammed the door shut to his soul. No wonder there were only darkness and bitterness within.

"Oh, oh," he cried out in remorse. "Pray for me, pray for me!"

"No!" was my startling reply. It stunned him like a shot from a rifle. "No! I will not pray for you now. You must pray for yourself. You know the truth. You are at a great divide in life!"

The next instant Ursula and I were transfixed as we saw the man suddenly slump down onto his knees in the middle of the room. Then there poured from his soul and from the depths of his spirit such a profound cry for mercy from Christ as I have seldom witnessed. Here was one under incredible conviction from God the Holy Spirit. Here was confession of sin such as is rarely heard. Here was genuine, godly repentance wrung from the very depths of a man's being.

It was but the beginning of an enormous renewal of an entire life. If ever there was a re-creation of character this was it. It was a living demonstration in tangible terms of an exquisite conversion and total restoration of an agnostic.

A few months later he and his wife decided to take a long tour visiting family and associates in the United States. Every few days a letter and postcards came back to us telling of the warm reception they received from people who previously wished he had never showed up. They could not believe the change.

One of these was his brother, the professor of music. He was also an avid collector of old violins. When he was told the story of how his belligerent brother had come to Christ, he walked across the room, lifted one of his most valued instruments from where it adorned the wall and handed it to him. "Here, take this back to that man Keller," he smiled. "It's worth it to see such a change in you!"

When, after weeks and weeks away, the couple came home, he rushed over to my home and placed the exquisite instrument in my hands. It was a rare violin of great vintage. But, sad to say, it had been hung on the wall unused for so long, its joints had begun to separate. I took it to a master violin maker. Almost in fear, with gentle reverence, he lifted it tenderly in his work-worn hands. "It is the most beautiful violin I have ever held. If you will allow me I can restore its song!" And he did, with loving care, and his master's touch. It came to have an exquisite tone.

A few months later this elderly man, whom Christ had so completely restored, went to open a window and fell dead in the presence of his wife. She came to see us. Instead of being torn with sorrow, she was tranquil and at peace. "The last three months we had together were absolute heaven. He was completely restored in the Master's hands!" she whispered softly.

I was invited to take part in his memorial service. When I did, the simple theme of my talk was to tell the lovely, moving story of how our Father picked up this broken, bitter man and gave him a new song. It was precisely the same way the old violin maker had picked up the ancient instrument and re-created its resonance.

Thank You, Father! How faithful You are!

It was not just elderly people whom Christ met and changed in our humble home. There were younger people as well. Some appeared outwardly successful. Yet within they were torn and fractured by the fragmentation of their families or the false and vain enticements of our sordid society.

One night after a class a sturdy young athletic coach came to me quietly and asked if we might have a private chat. He was a total stranger to me at the time. We had never met before. He was not a Christian nor at that point in time did he appear keen to become one.

Out of sheer desperation, at the urging of a friend, he had come to our home. He and his wife, both outstanding athletes in their own fields, he in field and track, she in tennis, had been very active on the local social scene. They were popular people with a wide circle of associates. Both had that sharp sparkle and keen energy so apparent in youth.

Then one day the attractive young lady, mother of two handsome children, became enamored of another gentleman whom she met in her tennis tournaments. One thing led to another, the relationship between the two became more involved, until suddenly on an impulse of allurement she left home, her husband, and her children. She fled to Europe with her new prince charming.

Her action shattered her husband. In dismay and anger, not knowing what to do, or where to turn, he finally showed up at our home. In firmness, honesty and compassion he was led to meet the Master who alone could bind up his broken hopes and heal his fractured home. I then urged him to extend the same sort of forgiveness to his delinquent wife as Christ Himself had shown to him despite the years of rebellion in his own life.

To my unbounded joy he found the courage to do this. In dogged determination he discovered where she was staying overseas; he called her long distance; he begged her to return, offering to forgive her freely; then he told of his own encounter with Christ.

She took the next plane home.

A few days later she too showed up at one of the classes. But there was a hard and brittle defiance to her attitude. Somewhere, somehow, in her past she had been wronged by church people. One night she told me privately that she would never, ever, be seen in any church. She had no use for such a thing. Yet strangely, surely, softly, Christ's Gracious Spirit was drawing her gently to Himself.

After several weeks I spoke to her again one night. "Why don't you go up into the high hills behind your home and get alone with our Father? Simply pour out your entire past to Him. Tell Him all. He knows it anyway and He understands you fully. Invite Him to speak to you, to touch you, to enter your life!"

She did just that. It proved to be a wondrous encounter between her and The Living Lord. In her life a total transformation took place. Old things were done away. Wonder of wonders for her, all things became new and fresh and satisfying.

In a gentle gesture of mutual good will and deep commitment, the two young people purchased brand new wedding bands to place upon each other's fingers. They became more firmly united than ever before as a family. Both of their children came to know Christ, and, unlikely as it ever seemed, they joined a local church.

The last occasion on which I visited that particular congregation it astonished me to be greeted at the door by this lovely lady. She, the one who had declared so firmly she would never be seen in any church, was now deeply involved.

Oh, the lovely changes Christ can make in human character.

Chapter 9

Learning Total Relinquishment to God's Will

Almost two full years had now elapsed since the awful heart-seizure in Australia. Little by little in gentle succession day upon day my physical stamina had increased. Without consulting any doctors or seeking any medical aid, but relying solely on my Father's care, I found my strength restored. My gratitude was like a deep spring of genuine praise and thanks welling up within my spirit.

In unflinching faith and calm confidence, I quietly claimed such superb commitments made for me as the ones in Psalm 103:1–4.

> *"Bless the Lord, O my soul:*
> *and all that is within me, bless his holy name.*
> *Bless the Lord, O my soul,*
> *and forget not all his benefits:*
> *who forgiveth all thine iniquities:*
> *who healeth all thy diseases:*
> *who redeemeth thy life from destruction:*
> *who crowneth thee with lovingkindness and*
> *tender mercies."*

In all this I had a part. With rigid self-discipline, I ate only beneficial foods in moderation, especially fresh fruit and vegetables. Some were grown in our garden which I dug and tended with care. Fruit came to us in abundance from friends who owned orchards. It touched us deeply to have neighbors drop in with baskets of cherries, apricots, apples and pears. All this was part of our Father's beautiful provision for us, passed gently to our home through their kind hands.

Every day, too, I tried without fail to engage in some modest physical exertion. I took long tramps along the lake. I climbed the hills. I dug the garden or mowed the lawn.

The stretching of muscles, the exercise of my aching chest, the exposure to clean, cool air, the warm touch of the sun day after day worked the wonder of health and healing in my body. Combined with all this was a regimen of regular rest and sound sleep. We retired early, for I have always been a man to rise long before dawn. It is then that I love to meet privately in solitude with my Master. It is in the hours of utter stillness, before break of day, that my mind is most acute and eager for long, intense thought. To make up for these early hours a nap after lunch became a regular habit. The quiet interlude of rest recharged my energy and gave new impetus to the balance of the day.

Lastly, by virtue of quiet determination, I slowly learned how to avoid undue stress. I know that some stress is essential to produce challenge and excitement in life which is good for the soul. But I refer here to those tensions and anxieties common to our human condition which wear men and women down with undue worry. Increasingly I learned in quiet trust to place my problems in my Father's hands and leave them there. I did not expect instant solutions, but I did find refreshing repose in the assurance He could resolve matters better than I could, in His own good time. So life took on a much more relaxed and joyous dimension. In all this there was a delightful renewal of spirit, soul and body. It was the unfolding of a brand new chapter in life.

But before that could be attained there still remained several formidable spiritual lessons I needed to learn in order to be totally available to my Father's purposes for me. The first was a need to understand complete relinquishment of my will to His. The second was to realize I was not to send down deep roots into any given spot.

About this time it astonished us to find that real estate values had suddenly started to escalate in the valley. I called in a friend who had great experience in the field and was surprised when he told us our home had virtually doubled in value since we bought it. He said it was an excellent time to sell if we wished to re-locate. The challenge was to find other property not yet risen in price.

My old, fierce love of the land had returned as my strength surged. And it seemed with renewed vigor I could once more handle a modest country estate. We decided to see what we might be able to find. To our surprise we came across a beautiful block of sixteen acres that resembled a bit of Switzerland. It lay high on a hill overlooking two lakes, magnificently secluded at the very end of a little winding country road. It had only a small fruit picker's cabin on it, but seven acres were planted in choice varieties of apricots, plums, apples and pears. It was not even for sale, but an old man who leased it told us he would soon retire and the absent owner might consider disposing of it.

I went to find the owner. Yes, he was thinking of selling. To my unbounded delight he quoted me a price about half of what most people asked. There was only $50.00 in my wallet that morning. I put it in his hand as a token of good faith. We drew up a simple agreement on a sheet of paper. And I was the owner of an orchard.

I rushed home to share the exciting development with Ursula. In our glee we went to a small cafe to celebrate the event. Our pastor's wife walked in just then. She had become a dear friend. When she saw me her immediate reaction was, "Phillip, what has happened? You look exactly like the cat that just swallowed the canary!" We all roared in laughter when I shared the good news of our new acquisition.

To our delight it was a simple matter to sell our home. We inserted a small advertisement in a large city paper. A few days later a couple appeared at the door, fell in love with the place and bought it outright.

Within a month Ursula and I had cleaned up the cabin on the hill. We installed a new wood heater, mowed the tall grass all around the place, and moved in to share the solitude with bears, deer, marmots and even a family of skunks whose den was under the cabin.

Because the terrain was so steep I had to have a special tractor built. It was fitted with dual wheels on an extra low chassis so it would not "turn turtle" on the dangerously steep slopes. Later I learned that three tractors had run away and smashed up on these dangerous acres. So orcharding here was much more than an ordinary challenge.

Somehow the remoteness of our location, the intoxicating beauty of our high, rugged hills above the lake, the wildlife that shared this upland world with us, all combined to make us feel we wanted to stay a long time. We drew plans for a lovely log chalet we would build on a huge rock outcrop overlooking the whole region. Just then we did not dream our Father had other things in mind for us entirely.

A few months later I was down in the orchard when I saw a man walking toward me in the shadows of the trees. It was the pastor of the church we attended in town. He was the precious fellow we had heard first on the radio in the camper years before—a man who truly knew and loved Christ. What a special person!

Without fanfare or formality he stated the reason for his visit. "Phillip, I have come to ask you to join me in the work of the church!" He smiled gently. "We need you to come and teach our people the Word of God."

On the surface it sounded so plausible, so inviting, so acceptable. But deep within my will and spirit it produced a startling reaction of disquiet and resentment. Instead of agreeing at once, I asked for time to consider such a serious responsibility.

Question after question surged through my soul. Doubts intruded into my mind. A stance almost of surprise, dismay and defiance swept into my spirit.

"Why didn't the church ask me to take this on before we left town? Why should they ask me now that I was high up in the hills with so much work on my hands? How could anyone be expected to handle both an orchard and church work? Surely my Father knew all about this offer. Why did He ever allow me to get caught in such a bind between this land on the hill and His work in the city?"

So the stormy struggle raged within. In a sense I was baffled by it all. Yet, despite my misgivings, I agreed to go down and work with the church as a lay pastor. I knew I could not do both jobs. The orchard would have to go. The land must be sold. All our dreams were blown away in the wind of these new events.

It was a fearsome time of inner turmoil.

I was determined to put our Father's work first.

But now the land was like a millstone around my neck.

There were nearly 700 trees to tend, to prune, to spray, to thin, to pick, to water with some 46 movable sprinklers. There were impossible steep acres to mow and work at incredible risk. There were tons and tons of fruit to take off the trees—12 tons of apricots alone. How did one feeble man do all this and still serve a rapidly growing church in the city?

More and more people were crowding into the Bible classes. We even had waiting lists. First there were two, then three, then four a week. There were services on Sunday. The work escalated everywhere. I felt trapped, caught in a net of exhausting demands.

In desperation, almost in dismay, we decided to sell the land. Again my real estate friend was asked to appraise the property. But this time things were totally different. When it was put on the market no one seemed interested. With the increasing lack of action there was also an increasing frustration in feeling caught between the escalating demands of the church work and the ever-present care of the fruit crop.

This inner turmoil began to degenerate into dark doubt as to whether my Father really cared. Then it turned to animosity because of the growing burden of responsibility. Little did I realize that it was my own tough intransigence, my own steel will set against God's good will, that was providing the impasse, preventing His Spirit from working freely in the situation.

Then one blazing hot morning it happened. I was out in the orchard all alone moving the 46 sprinklers. Lifting my spirit in a profound act of complete capitulation to Christ, I stood erect and spoke to Him audibly: "Oh, my Master, if You wish me to remain on this place the rest of my days and serve You in this way I will! If You wish me to pour out my energy and risk my life on these steep slopes, I do so gladly. If You desire me to expend my strength on caring for this orchard and moving these sprinklers to the end of my days, I accept Your wishes."

It was the most sincere prayer of utter relinquishment I had ever made in my life. I was absolutely sincere. With it went the anger, the frustration, the doubts and despair within. I was a man set free!

Within four days of that very hour, four buyers suddenly appeared—one from Sweden, one from Switzerland, one from Texas and one from Alberta. The place was sold at once for the full price, all cash, twice what we paid. I had also learned my Father did not expect me to put down deep roots in any earthly spot. Thank You, Father!

There had been several lovely compensations made to us during our days up on the hill. One had been the number of people whose lives had been totally transformed through coming to the classes and there meeting Christ. Of these some became dear friends and loving associates who were to enrich our lives for the rest of our days.

The other compensation was a handsome big Malamute given to us by a couple who had owned him for twelve years. Though he was advanced in age, still "Shep" brought with him a buoyancy of spirit and fund of great good cheer that enlivened our days and filled them with fun. He took to us at once and became a beloved companion who roamed all over the place with me.

Shep had more than his share of excitement with the bears which came in to pick up the fallen fruit under the trees. He challenged the marmots on the rocks who loved to feast on our drying apricots. He had more than one run-in with the skunks on the hill. And he stood watch against any strangers who ever set foot on our land.

I had never seen a dog who tried so hard to actually "talk" to us in low guttural sounds that conveyed his joys and concerns. Just by his behavior I could always tell if anyone had come while we were away. He was a loyal friend.

He loved snow with a passion. He ran, rolled and tumbled in it with the glee and gaiety of a child. His dark, thick coat shone with rich luster in winter weather. And his handsome face bore a perpetual smile.

He was the only dog I ever knew who could "pray." He would sit beside us, place his two paws up on my thigh, then bury his head between his outstretched legs. If he dared look up, like a bad boy, we would whisper: "No peeking!" Down would go his head in further prayer. Strange to say, his prayers were always answered, for they never once failed to produce a delicious tidbit for him. I learned much from him.

Chapter 10

Deep Decisions

Selling our lovely land up in the hills was to be a "great divide" in life. That painful experience brought into sharp focus the formidable fact that from now on my Master would see fit to move me many times to various locations to serve His people. By degrees there was being borne in upon my spiritual awareness that I really was not my own boss. I belonged to Christ, and I was a man under command. Completely available to His authority, I was to be prepared to pack up and move into any arena of action He called me to enter.

This is not an easy way to live, especially when one's friends and family regard such a lifestyle as unpredictable and somewhat shiftless. Often Ursula and I were regarded as gypsies or "ne'r-do-wells" who simply drifted about from one place to another—a bit like dandelion seeds blown by the wind. In one very real sense this was an apt simile. We were indeed moved hither and yon by the impulse of the Wind of God's Gracious Spirit. It was He who picked us up and set us down in all sorts of spots. And often this was hard for others to understand.

For me as a man it proved a great adventure in discovering the ongoing faithfulness of my Master. Invariably He had a place prepared for us in advance. And He would lead us to it with remarkable excitement. It was He who would then enable us to bloom and flourish wherever He chose to plant us for a spell. For all of this I was deeply grateful to Him. Because He made the decisions, we were spared from serious mistakes. Blessing upon blessing followed every move we made. Lives were touched for Christ that would otherwise not have known His love. Books were written that would not have come to life. And God's work was advanced in wondrous ways all over the earth.

There was a price to pay in all of this. It meant that we had to live very frugally. There was the constant need to keep one's possessions to an absolute minimum. One had to learn to travel lightly through life, not weighed down or encumbered with excessive baggage or personal belongings. Whatever we owned was held in an open hand, readily shared with anyone in need, given without grudging to those we met on the twisting trails of life.

Our lives did not consist in the abundance of things which we possessed nor in the comfort of our accommodation. Rather, the measure of their depth was gauged by the people we impacted and the gracious good Christ saw fit to accomplish in their experience.

Even in this there was an element of stern sacrifice, for many of these precious people became dear friends. Nor is it easy to pull up stakes and part from those who have become fond of us. It might have been much, much easier and more comfortable just to settle down softly in some cozy corner surrounded by one's intimate associates. But it was not to be if we were going to obey the Master's call.

So now again that call had come unmistakably. We would return to live in the heart of town. It was my strong conviction that the physical strength and buoyant energy restored to me should be expended for the benefit of others, not my own pleasure or pursuits. I was determined to give myself unstintingly to the people who were coming into the classes and into the church in increasing numbers.

These folk came from every sort of background and almost every strata of society. The great central attraction that drew them together was the exaltation of Christ as God very God. As they came to know Him, to trust Him, to love Him, to serve Him, they were drawn together in powerful bonds of mutual loyalty. It was wonderful to see the transformation in so many lives. For the young pastor and myself it was a great adventure with God.

We were like two blood brothers caught up together in an exciting enterprise of divine design. Really, it was that. There was an element of harmony, good will, mutual cooperation and eager enthusiasm seldom seen in church work. It spilled over to the dear people we served so that on every hand there was the distinct impression that Christ was with us in wondrous ways of His own arrangement.

About this same time the few devotional books I had written began to attract an ever-widening audience. Presumably, this was simply because one reader would tell another. Virtually nothing had been done to try and promote the books. Publishers of Christian books regarded me as an "unknown" layman. And with my personal aversion to publicity of any sort, I was not prepared to hit the lecture trail, as so many authors do, in an attempt to promote my own work.

This led to another deep decision in my life. I determined then that my complete confidence would reside in Christ to use the books to honor Himself. It was He who would enrich, uplift and touch others through them. Thus one reader would tell another. In this way the works would become well known. So eventually people all over the earth could benefit from the books. In a word my

Master could be trusted to take and bless the work of writing to millions upon millions of readers.

Subsequent events proved His utter faithfulness in this. A surprising number of simple books, written in layman's language that common people could readily understand, became national and international best sellers. They were published in an ever-increasing number of foreign tongues all over the world until today they have been translated into some twenty-six different languages. All of this left me in awe. I could only bow my head and heart to whisper fervently, "Thank You, Father!"

This development, though profoundly rewarding, posed somewhat of a dilemma. As the books became well known, publishers began to take an increased interest in this "unknown" man living in a distant mountain valley of rugged British Columbia. In my wildest dreams it had never entered my mind that Emerson's immortal lines would ever be true of me:

"If a man write a better book; preach a better sermon; or build a better mousetrap than his neighbor, though he build his house in the woods, the world will make a beaten path to his door." (Ralph Waldo Emerson, 1803–1882)

Yet this was the case.

Editor after editor traveled from the great publishing houses of the east to try to find me tucked away in my mountain hideaways. This rather amused me for the simple reason that they seemed startled to find a man living in such simplicity in such a down-to-earth manner.

What from my perspective posed the most weighty consideration was not where I lived or how I worked, but rather how my time was to be divided between serving the people of the local church and the wider audience of readers throughout the world. I am not a person who can handle several tasks at the same time, well. I am very single minded, capable of enormous concentration, with all my capacities addressed to a single project at one time. The aim is to produce the finest result possible. This applies whether the enterprise be writing books, preparing a lecture, developing a ranch or studying the life habits of a Bighorn Ram.

So the ever-intensifying demand for more books came into competition with the ever more compelling responsibilities of a steadily growing church. Though the latter were kind enough to grant me time off for writing, the ever mounting pressures of the two enterprises began to take their toll.

This first began to make itself apparent in the loss of my memory. At first this was dismissed with a shrug of the shoulders and a hearty chuckle. Just a sign of advancing age! Or perhaps it was simply a case where my mental computer was overloaded and needed a little more time to clear itself. Still, the problem persisted and became alarmingly acute. I was gradually moving into a condition of confusion where it was obvious I simply did not have the clear, concise control previously enjoyed and taken so much for granted.

The second serious symptom that alerted me to my dilemma was an increasing occurrence of ferocious head pains. These were not migraine headaches, but tremendous stress and tension pressures from trying to handle two responsibilities at the same time. It was obvious I could no longer carry both loads.

In great earnestness of spirit and sincerity of soul I sought guidance from my Father as to what I should do. It became ever more clear that a deep decision had to be made which would radically affect the rest of my life.

One quiet, calm morning I went to walk alone along the lake shore. Every hill, tree, bulrush and rock were reflected in the shining surface like a mirror. I besought my Father what course I should take. What work should I pursue? What responsibilities should I relinquish?

Suddenly, sharply, as clearly as if articulated in human language, the question leaped into my awareness:

"What influence have I used to teach you the greatest lessons in life—books or ministers?"

Without a second's hesitation my response was—*"Books!"*

Then just as emphatically the assurance came to me, *"Then books are to be your priority for the present. You will write them for Me to reach people all over the earth!"*

In that instant my main life work was decided. I was at peace. The inner conflict was gone. Thank You, Father!

Without delay I went to share this decision with my colleague. He was a gentle man of great heart. In profound sincerity he simply replied: "Phillip, if that is our Father's choice for you, we will accept it. He knows best. He will bless you in writing books!"

Our years together had been tremendously joyous, hearty and stimulating. They had been extremely valuable in showing me first hand the challenges faced by pastors in our decadent society and crude culture. Not only had Christ used the years to touch others, but also to deepen us in our devotion to Himself. My work had taken me into homes, hospitals, jails, psychiatric wards and hovels where drugs and poverty and drunkenness were a way of life. Yet everywhere we went we also saw the majestic power of The Most High prevail over the evil and degradation of lost men and women in despair.

It did not matter what condition people were in. Again and again we were thrilled and overjoyed to see them meet the Master. What wondrous changes Christ brought about in their lives! What new and vibrant people they became!

Still the leaving was not easy. In quietness we searched for another spot to live where most of my time could be given to writing. At last we stumbled on a tiny cabin beside a quiet little lake. We called it "Still Waters." Its story has been told in the book by the same name. It was a precious place of great serenity. Within its humble walls were written some of the most well-loved books I ever wrote: *Walking with God, A Gardener Looks at the Fruits of the Spirit, Gideon—Man of Valour.*

In those days I felt driven by my deteriorating physical condition. In a peculiar way it seemed death was imminent. The bad days with excruciating head pains outnumbered the good days. With intense zeal I wrote and wrote whenever I was well enough to put pen to paper.

This is not a mere play on words. I do not know how to type. I am such a primitive person I cannot "think" through any mechanical mechanism. Everything is written by hand, using an old-fashioned fountain pen. In that way the thoughts and impulses imparted to me by my Father flow directly onto the paper. And once put into visible word form on the sheet, they are scarcely ever altered. There simply are no second or third drafts. The book manuscript is typed out by Ursula exactly as I wrote it, without any re-writing.

There is only one drawback to this simple procedure. Good fountain pens are exceedingly difficult to come by in this age of the computer and word processor. I have to send as far away as New Zealand or Great Britain to find instruments suited to my Father's work.

Fortunately I have found several select editors who respect my work enough that they do not try to change or "edit" its content. They seem to recognize that in reality it is my Father who is the author of the work in hand, and as of old I am but His scribe—the one who transfers to paper the profound convictions He imparts to my mind and soul and spirit by His Spirit. In this He is ever faithful to me.

Morning after morning, long before dawn, as I quiet my soul before His Majesty, my Most High Sovereign, I claim His noble and wondrous commitments to me:

> *"Fear thou not; for I am with thee:*
> *be not dismayed for I am thy God;*

I will strengthen thee;
Yea, I will help thee;
Yea, I will uphold thee with the right hand
of my righteousness." Isaiah 41:10

This He has done with never-ending faithfulness. And today, some twelve years later, He has completely restored my health, my memory, my capacity to serve Him fully. *Thank You, Father!*

Chapter 11

Santa Barbara Again

The wee cabin beside the lake was a choice spot for most of the year. But it had not been built or designed for use in Canada's severe winters. Its walls were not insulated; its great expanses of glass lost too much heat; its primitive plumbing was too vulnerable to the frigid temperatures.

Nor was I inclined to expend my limited strength and marginal energy shoveling snow, splitting wood and thawing out pipes when other much more important work could be accomplished. So we decided to spend the winters in the south. Some twenty years before I had studied photography at The Brooks Institute of Photography in Santa Barbara, California. It impressed me then as a choice seaside community with a lovely climate where one's health could improve. Also, the natural beauty of the area combined with its unusual geographical ambience of mountains and seascapes produced a stimulating, creative location in which an author could work with vigor.

There was one formidable obstacle to going there again. It had become one of the most affluent cities in the nation. The cost of accommodation was prohibitive—so much so that it seemed unlikely we would ever establish a home of our own there. Still, in quiet faith, we were sure our Father could lead us to a suitable spot of His arrangement if He wanted us there. For the first few winters we simply stayed in low-cost rental accommodation. This was not always very desirable. Wild night parties, drunken neighbors, smashed vehicles were all a common part of the social scene. They were vivid reminders of the rough, tough culture of California, a state not highly rated in social niceties (in some areas at least!).

Very quickly we became acutely aware that we were in one of the world's great mission fields. On one hand were the richest of the rich. On the other were tough transients.

It never ceased to astonish me how extremely wealthy many of the families were who lived in this community. Residential areas such as Montecito and Hope Ranch claimed a large number of millionaires and multimillionaires. When in due course I began to hold Bible study sessions throughout the city it intrigued me to discover how preoccupied these people were with their possessions and personal security. One could only assume that having accumulated huge assets they were now afraid of losing their riches.

In subsequent years I often remarked jokingly: "God called Mother Teresa to minister to the poorest of the poor. He called me to minister to the richest of the rich." And, of the two, as Jesus told us, the latter were much less likely to respond to the overtures of His concern. How few wealthy people ever came fully under Christ's control!

One of the great benefits that accrued from our time in California was the steady, sure improvement in my health. Little by little my memory began to be restored. No doubt the serenity of the seaside, the long strolls along the beaches, the less strenuous demands of my daily work habits all combined to heal my overworked mind. My powers of intense concentration and clear thought control returned with fresh force and exhilarating vigor. All this would become clearly evident in books such as *Mountain Splendor, Ocean Glory, Rabboni, Wonder o' the Wind* and *Sea Edge.*

In all this creative enterprise I was acutely aware that it was essentially Christ's precious presence which made it all possible. It was His life, His energy, His inspiration, His motivation within my soul and spirit that enabled the work to proceed. For my part there was the inescapable awareness that in utter humility I could do all things through Him. For this I was deeply grateful. *Thank You, Father!*

During this interval of time, invitations began to come for me to address various conferences and conventions. It surprised me that this would be so. Just because an author produces books that have a wide appeal does not mean he must by the same measure be a suitable speaker. Some writers are bound to be tongue-tied standing before an audience, while the very thought of making public appearances is enough to terrify those who are timid.

This new dimension to life was something I needed to examine carefully. There is a great danger in it if the author uses it as a means to promote his own popularity or to advertise his own work and skills. I simply refused to let this happen. Full well I knew that any success the books enjoyed was because of my Master's special stamp of approval upon the work He and I had accomplished together. I was not about to take personal honor from that achieved under His direction.

Bit by bit certain specific disciplines of self-conduct were established for speaking engagements accepted.

1) By careful prayer and meditation it had to be determined that in fact the invitation was in accordance with His will. Put another way, I had to be sure a specific audience had its spiritual needs to meet, and that the whole exercise was not just a stunt to promote some

program or titillate some curious people. Many invitations were not accepted!

2) I would go only to speak of Christ and His great redemptive purposes for His children. It was God our Father who would be honored. Any message delivered came from Him. I was there with a word from on High. I refused to discuss my own work or to promote my own books.

3) There must be absolute freedom to let God's Spirit select the subjects which should be dealt with in the services. He alone knew the themes best suited to the audience I faced.

4) For my part, I trusted my Father not only to give me the messages, but also the courage to deliver them without fear or reservation.

As a footnote to all this I had to trust Him implicitly for His presence and strength to meet the strangers and adversities of travel which such work entailed. By nature I am a solitary man. Meeting strangers and mingling with crowds are difficult for me. Being in the public eye is abhorrent, so serving in this manner called for, and still does, enormous self-sacrifice. Often I felt very much like a lamb led to its own death at the hands of a fickle public. Only my Father's presence could sustain me under such stress. Still, if there were needy, lost men and women to reach I dare not hold back. I would simply go for His sake and purposes.

Added to all the foregoing was the strain of unknown travel emergencies. These came in a hundred different guises. A whole book could be written just about the hair-raising episodes I encountered in getting back and forth to various engagements. Here again I had to rely completely, in quiet faith, upon my Father to care for me amid all the confusion and complexities of twentieth century travel.

So that the reader can understand a little of what this work for God involves, let me recount here the highlights of just one engagement. Then you will understand why my experiences as a convention speaker were not all just fun and games.

Arrangements had been made for me to take a full week of services at a large Christian conference in Houston, Texas. Upon arrival in that oil city I was billeted in a rather shabby motel in a seedy section of the sprawling town. The first room I was given was adjacent to the huge air-conditioning unit that roared incessantly. Sleep was impossible, so I requested another room. The staff were less than cordial and showed me to a room where the lights did not work and the plumbing was faulty. I am not a man with delicate tastes. I have roughed it all over the world under tough conditions. But, as if to intimidate me, the staff warned me not to go out to walk alone after dark in that neighborhood. I was bound to be knifed or attacked by hoodlums. This was hardly reassuring since the convention center was a half-hour walk away—and I had not been provided with "wheels" to get back and forth.

I walked anyway, trusting Christ to care for me!

The services were all well attended by both black and white people. To my surprise, not a single white family invited me to their home—possibly because of deep prejudice against anyone born and raised in Africa. So most of my meals were eaten alone in a crummy cafe near the motel. To reach it I risked going back and forth across the twilight zone at all hours.

Finally, near the end of the week, a magnificent, portly black lady with a shining face asked if I would care to come to her home. I was glad to go. I love black people! She squeezed her handsome frame into a tiny Volkswagen "Bug," with me by her side. We roared twenty-three miles out to her tiny home on the outskirts of the city.

On the way she explained her place was crowded with a jobless family—two adults and two teenagers—whom she had taken in off the streets. Houston was in dire depression then. No work was available. Times were tough! Texas was in turmoil.

We sat down to a simple meal of boiled rice and wild mustard greens gathered from vacant land. Yet for me it was a banquet prepared with love, shared with a compassionate spirit. During the meal I suggested we entreat our Father to supply work for at least one of the family.

My dear hostess then took me to her bedroom and insisted I have a little siesta to refresh me for the evening service. I slept in great serenity.

Soon after I awakened the phone rang. It was the local hospital calling the unemployed mother to report for duty the next morning. Unabashed jubilation filled that cottage. Thank You, Father! We drove back to the church in glee.

From then on the services were crowded with joyous black people who sang with unbounded enthusiasm and gratitude to God. They took me to themselves as though I were indeed one of their own. What precious people they were, deeply touched and moved by the mercy of The Most High.

At last the final day came. My flight back to California was due to depart about an hour after the morning service concluded. An elderly gray-haired man asked if he could drive me to the airport. I accepted his offer with joy.

But this delight turned to doubt when he led me out to his fire-engine-red sports car without a roof. He informed me he was a newcomer to Houston and did not know where the airport was—did I? With only the vaguest idea of where to go he roared off down a nearby freeway, his hair blowing wildly in the wind.

Twice we took off-ramps to inquire where the airport was. Twice we found gas station attendants who were as ignorant as ourselves. Then, just in time, with only minutes to spare, my heart racing, we roared into the airport and I caught my plane by a mere eyelash.

We flew west until suddenly over the desert wastes of Arizona the plane suddenly began to circle slowly in the hot sun, going nowhere. The captain came on the speaker to announce that dense coastal fog over Los Angeles had backed up air traffic for hundreds of miles.

Eventually we crossed the coast range and began our descent down into the pea soup overcast moving in off the Pacific. At first I wondered if a safe landing was possible. As we made our approach an acute atmosphere of tension gripped the whole aircraft.

My seatmate was a worried black woman. As her anxiety mounted so did the beads of perspiration rising over her face and forehead. "Oh, Lordie, Lordie!" she kept ejaculating. "Oh, Lordie, Lordie!" She drew a small Testament from her purse and opened it feverishly. I leaned over toward her gently. "Lady, if you truly know Him, just trust Him!" I whispered in her ear. "He can care for us!" Just then there was a heavy thud and our wheels were on the landing strip. We were down safely, rolling steadily to a stop.

By now dark had descended. The connecting flights to Santa Barbara had long since left. I and a scattering of other passengers were simply stranded there, facing the prospect of sleeping away the night sitting up in the smoke-filled waiting room. And of course at home my wife would be wondering whatever happened and where in the world I could be.

Suddenly an energetic young Irishman with a lilting accent came up to me. Would I be interested in renting a car and sharing expenses if he drove us up to Santa Barbara, a hundred miles away? I was not at all sure I wanted, or needed, a second hair-raising ride with a total stranger on this tempestuous day. However, giving his offer a moment's thought I quickly agreed on the condition he get the car and at least one other passenger.

To my surprise he soon came back, not only with a car, but also two other passengers besides myself. The four of us, all total strangers, piled into the vehicle with our baggage. The talkative Irishman wheeled out onto the freeway and headed north in high spirits.

To my unbounded relief he knew every turn in the road. With skill and ease he sped toward Santa Barbara. In a flourish of good will he deposited us at the quiet little airport. There Ursula awaited me with joy, for I had phoned her I was coming. But I felt ten years older than when I had left home a week before.

Chapter 12

Beside the Sea

Season followed season. Year followed year. Gradually it became ever more difficult to find a suitable spot to stay each winter. More people were moving into this placid little seaside town; property values were escalating; accommodation was becoming more expensive and the only sensible thing was to try to find a modest home suited to our simple needs.

Ursula and I have taken seriously the stewardship of all that our Father entrusts to our care. Across the years we have lived simply and without show. Always the main aim has been to share what came to us with those whose needs were greater than our own. This has been true not only for the poor and destitute on this continent who came across our path, but also for those in need overseas far from our shores.

So the funds available for our own homes were always somewhat seriously restricted. This meant we had to rely on our Father to lead us to places He had in mind for us. The search in Santa Barbara was just as strenuous and exciting as had been the one when we first returned to Canada from overseas.

We came to know two real estate couples well. Both were superb man-and-wife teams active in the field. In spite of their most concerted efforts on our behalf, nothing suitable opened up for us. Yet it really was not a wasted effort. For one day as we drove home from looking at properties the one lady said to me, "There is something unusual about you. You have a serene spirit amid all this searching. Are you a Christian?"

I assured her I was. Moreover I said it would be a special pleasure to introduce her to Christ. She invited us to her home that evening for a quiet chat.

Little did I know that though she was a person seeking, yearning, longing to know spiritual truth, her husband was not . . . at least at this point in his life. It turned out to be a somewhat stormy episode in their home that evening. While I sat on the couch, trying gently to explain to the lovely lady of the house exactly what it meant to become a Christian, her hostile husband sat defiantly in one corner of the room glaring at me in anger.

Every once in a while he would break into the quiet conversation with a wild denunciation, such as: "That is just a myth" — or — "Christianity is just a crutch for weak people to lean on" — or — "Who needs to believe all that stuff?"

I was not to be intimidated by his belligerent outbursts. Steadfastly, without rancor, I went on to explain how Christ came to deliver us from our bondage to sin, to ourselves and to Satan, our arch foe. In Him there was freedom, forgiveness and the wondrous joy of belonging to the family of God, our Father.

At the time it seemed as if there was no emphatic response to the good news of our Father's love for them. But a few days later the lady phoned to say she was giving her whole life to Christ in complete capitulation. She begged us to pray earnestly for her husband.

I took this request seriously and promised to do so faithfully. In a few days we were returning north and would not see them again for about six months.

The very first day we returned I called their home. It was the husband who answered the phone. "Oh, Phillip, Phillip!" he shouted jubilantly. "I have become a Christian! I'm attending a men's Bible study. I'll come around tomorrow and take you to it!"

I almost dropped the phone in astonishment. What marvelous good news. How gracious my Father had been!

Today that dear, dear couple are precious friends. In His mercy and compassion Christ has bound us together in His wondrous family. Thank You, Father!

Ursula and I finally concluded that if our agents were unable to find us a home, this did not mean our Father could not locate one for us. So we began to search quietly on our own.

One evening we went to walk softly amongst a group of condominiums built beside the sea. It was a lovely location with immediate access to a beautiful beach. But as was true of so many developments of this kind, all the units were sold; the doors were all shut; and an air of seclusion surrounded the scene.

I screwed up my courage and invited Ursula to come with me for a walk through. "If I see anyone I will ask if they know of anything for sale," I remarked softly. "Who knows what we might find here!"

We strolled past door after door, all closed, all locked, all forbidding entrance. Suddenly we came to a garage door wide open. I peered into the gloomy interior. A man was hunched over the engine of his car, half buried from sight by the upraised hood. I dared to walk in, my pulse pounding.

"Excuse me, sir, for interrupting you as a total stranger." The sound of my voice startled him. He looked up rather defiantly, taken aback by my audacity. Still I went on, "We just wondered if you might know of anyone here who would consider selling their condominium?"

For a few moments he did not speak or reply at

all. Then staring at me sternly he simply lifted two outstretched fingers, pointed upward to the ceiling of the garage. I was puzzled by his gesture. What did it mean? I pressed him to explain.

"Yes!" he grunted, "Just last night I decided to sell!"

He went on to explain that the unit was in disarray. It had not been tidied up for showing to the public. His wife, an airline stewardess, was away on a flight. So the place was not presentable. Still, if we were seriously interested, he would show us through. We said we were, so he wiped the oil and grease from his work-stained hands and led us into his home.

It was exactly what we wanted! The great glass windows and doors had glorious views of the breakers on the beach. It had room enough that I could have a study to work in. The whole place pulsed with light and good cheer.

I asked him his price. He had not settled that fully but quoted me a ballpark figure that took my breath away. It was within our reach if a deal could be struck. I agreed to come back three days later after his wife returned. It would give us a second look, though we did not need it. It would also give them time to make a final decision on price and terms.

To our unbounded delight they stuck to the original price quoted. And when we offered to let them stay for several months, until they found a new place for themselves, they were elated.

Only one rather important matter remained. Could we get all the money together in time to pay them out in full, all cash, without incurring any debts? In this we had to trust our Father without flinching. I assured the owners I would meet them at 5:00 P.M. exactly ten days later to confirm that we had all the cash in hand.

Gently but confidently we placed the entire transaction in Christ's care, assured that He could supply what was needed. At 2:00 P.M. of the day that the deal was to be closed a wire came stating one of my publishers in the east had just remitted enough money to my bank in Santa Barbara to more than pay for the place. We were jubilant. At last we had a home in California. What a thrill!

Step by step, surely, serenely, without fanfare or fuss or frustration, our Father had brought us to this delightful place of His appointment for us. A profound sense of peace, contentment and quiet well-being enfolded our spirits.

When the final transaction was completed by the escrow officer, the remark made was most telling: "This is the most simple, straightforward, delightful sale I have ever concluded in Santa Barbara." All of it was a beautiful reminder of our Father's exquisite care.

Since I am a keen outdoorsman, our location beside the sea, and next door to a local bird refuge, provided the natural balance needed in my work as a writer and lecturer. It was a short climb over the garden wall, and in minutes I was on the sweeping sands of the shore. Here I could stroll for miles, away from the clamor and noise of the city. It was a stretch of beach of unusual beauty and diversity shared with hundreds of sea birds, sea lions and other denizens of the deep.

Not only did such a setting provide enormous solitude and inspiration, but steadily and surely it began to restore my body and mind from the stress and strain of so much responsibility. The good days began to outnumber the bad ones when my head throbbed with so much pain. Without seeking the aid of doctors or medical science I was being restored in wondrous ways. Because of this it was possible to begin Bible classes in the community for any who cared to attend. How grateful I was for my Father's healing touch upon my life. His presence, His companionship, His enthusiasm renewed and revitalized all of life. A fresh sense of adventure and new advances permeated my thinking.

In His exquisite understanding of my needs as a man

He was providing the dynamic for new creative work. Bless His name!

One of the long-range decisions which we had to make about this time was the disposal of the little lakeside cottage we lovingly called "Still Waters." It was some 1300 miles away to the north. Though kind friends kept an eye on the place, it ceased to be practical to keep it when we lived so far away. Then suddenly one spring I felt strongly constrained to go up and sell it.

To our astonishment we had scarcely opened the door when the phone rang. It was an elderly neighbor whom I had led to Christ several years before. How he had come to love his Lord! He even began to play an active role as a lay speaker in the little church he attended. He urged us to have the property carefully appraised by a local agent before we sold it, for I had offered it to several interested friends at exactly the price we paid for it. Not one would take us up on the offer.

So I called up my old associate who came out to look at the land. To our amazement he carefully appraised it at well over $50,000.00 more than we had paid for it. Ursula and I were taken aback. We had no idea land had escalated to this extent during our absence. What was even more remarkable, the first client shown the cottage purchased it on the spot, full price, all cash, payable within thirty days. It was almost like a fairy tale—except we knew it was our Father's gentle arrangement for us.

As added evidence of His special care, we faced one special little test of our faith in Him before our departure. It began to rain and rain and rain! This was unusual in such dry desert country. Every slope and streambed shed flooding waters into our little lake. Its level rose dangerously. The lake began to flood over the lawns, over the rockeries. I brought in hundreds of sandbags. Loving friends came out to help me build barricades, but the waters could not be kept back. Would the buyer retract on his purchase?

We asked our agent to be honest and open in advising the new owner of the flood damage. His reply was a hearty laugh! He knew the extent of the flooding. He was not at all concerned! He was just so glad to get the property we could relax in peace. A few days later the water levels would return to normal.

This spot had provided us with many a hearty laugh. One night friends were visiting when a beautiful, gentle, little white-footed mouse ran across the front room. Instead of becoming highly alarmed by the wee visitor we picked up the binoculars to examine him more closely. Our guests could not suppress their mirth: "Now we have seen everything, even to studying mice with field glasses in one's own front room!"

On another occasion a young friend, training for the ministry, offered to mow the lawns and care for the grounds while we were away. He was agitated when a big old buck beaver began to come ashore and cut down our ornamental trees. His best efforts to wrap the trees with wire netting did not deter the depredation.

Finally he decided to ambush the beaver. Seeing him coming across the lake, he crouched down behind the shrubbery. Then when the animal landed, the young pastor stalked him on hands and knees. Finally, with a loud shout and wild flourish of arms, he leaped at the hapless beaver, hoping to frighten him off forever.

Our next door neighbor was not aware of the beaver. Unknown to the young man, she had watched his antics from her balcony overlooking our lawn and reported the whole incident to us. Her closing comment was: "I knew he was a religious young fellow, but, really, I didn't know he was such a wild fanatic!" We laughed until our ribs ached.

It was with quiet repose but happy, happy memories that we left that lovely spot. Both of us brushed a few tears from our eyes.

Chapter 13

Productive Days

The years that followed our move to California remain as some of the most significant and productive in my life. Though I was now well into my sixties, an age at which most men consider the more comfortable years of retirement, my output of energy and work was steady, sustained by the very life of The Most High.

Part of the secret was that with advancing years I had learned to pace myself. One could not possibly meet all the demands for one's time. But allowing The Gracious Spirit of God to direct in daily decisions, I found it possible to accomplish a great deal in quiet, calm order. It was not a matter of "how much" was done, but rather a case of "how well" the work was done. Always, the ultimate aim was to please my Master and produce that which would enrich others. So the end result would be work of enduring worth.

This was also a time of special and unique growth in my own personal faith in God, my Father. Little by little I was learning to have implicit confidence in Christ, not only for the larger issues in life, but also for the minute details of daily living. Increasingly there stole over my spirit an acute awareness that I really was "a man under command," subject to the benign sovereignty of God's Guiding Spirit.

As I recount several very diverse events that occurred during this time the reader will understand what is meant. In this way it is possible to see how delightful and dramatic implicit faith in our Father can be.

Ursula and a friend had decided to attend the Christmas concert at Disneyland, about 120 miles away. The other lady had offered to drive them down in her rather battered old Volkswagen. It was to be a happy little adventure for the two ladies who regarded it as a lark.

It was early morning when the Volkswagen came swinging into the circular driveway in front of our home. None of the windows or windshield had been cleaned properly, so I asked the two excited ladies to wait about ten minutes while I cleaned all the glass carefully. They needed clear visibility to drive over 100 miles in heavy freeway traffic.

As they drove off in a roar, I waved to them happily. Then suddenly I looked down at the pavement where the vehicle had just stood. A large, dark pool of hot oil lay stark upon the asphalt. The engine leaked! Under high speed highway driving, the motor would normally run dry, then seize up.

But by this time they were long gone. There was no way to warn them of their impending danger and possible imminent disaster. Standing alone in the cool, brisk, winter morning air I immediately lifted my spirit to my Father. In simple entreaty I said: "Father, I place them in Your care. Protect them with Your presence. Preserve them from this great peril."

With joyous abandon the two ladies drove nonstop all the way to their motel in Disneyland. Just as they drew into their parking space Ursula's friend remembered for the first time that her husband had warned her to check the oil from time to time. When she did now, it was to discover that the engine was dry. No oil whatever showed on the dipstick.

Her husband had placed extra quarts of oil in the trunk of the vehicle. To come home the next day they had to stop several times along the way, and they used up more than four quarts of extra oil to get there.

This was a moving incident in more ways than one. Above all else, it inspired me to have ever increasing faith in my Father's care for His children. Today, just as in the time of Elijah, He could provide oil for those in need of it.

The second astonishing demonstration of our Father's care was in connection with the production of a film based on my book, *Lessons from a Sheep Dog*. I was somewhat reticent about such a project since I had no experience playing a role of this sort. But I was assured it would be low key without undue stress.

The basic plan was to do the film in two segments. The main narration would be in a large church with a full audience in attendance. This would be intercut with dramatic scenes from the second segment filmed high in the Rocky Mountains of Colorado with a bona fide sheep rancher's flock.

We arrived at the church several hours in advance of the shooting session. The film director decided my polyester shirt was creating too much static on the screen. It would have to be replaced by a cotton shirt. A friend and I went in search of such a garment only to find the best we could come up with was only 50 percent cotton. I bought it anyway.

Later when I returned to the preparation rooms the make-up man, in great alarm, exclaimed, "You're so dark! You will look black on the screen! I've got to lighten you up!" With that he proceeded to take a powder puff and pat a layer of white make-up all over my deeply tanned face, neck and hands. It was a disconcerting ordeal for me as a man, and I began to wish I had never agreed to the film project.

I was then passed on to a huge, tall Texan who said his job was "to wire me for sound." This involved strapping a pair of electronic transmitters to my body. He seemed to have endless difficulty adjusting them properly. His anxiety began to be transferred to me.

Then I was asked to go into the main sanctuary where the film crew wished to run several test shots to see if all was in order. To their consternation my newly purchased shirt seemed to create havoc on the monitor. Already people were pouring into the auditorium, among them my wife with several friends.

In desperation the director asked if I had brought any other shirts. I replied I had a frayed old bush shirt with me. Perhaps it would do? They rushed out and got it while the make-up man feverishly applied even more powder to my face. No, even the old bush shirt would not serve! Meanwhile, both Ursula in the audience, and I on the podium, died by degrees from all the alarm.

As a last resort the camera crew swung their cameras out over the swelling congregation in search of a suitable shirt. Ah, at last they found one on a tall lanky fellow! Without embarrassment the director went over and asked if he would consider swapping shirts with me. Surprisingly, he agreed!

Now again, back to the make-up room. By now all the crew were caught up in a sort of frantic frenzy. I was stripped down to my waist and faced the stranger with the cotton shirt. Handing him mine, I remarked rather dryly, "At least it is brand new!" His was not!

In the midst of this mayhem tempers flared; crew members began to insult each other; charges and countercharges were hurled at one another. Finally I decided to act in quiet faith. Turning to those around me I spoke firmly but softly. "This is our Father's work. He will enable us to pull it off properly. Please apologize to each other. Let us get on with the production."

Once more fully attired, I was prepared to go on the platform and make my presentation. Water was to have been provided for my parched throat. But amid all the confusion this was overlooked and forgotten. Again I assured the staff. "It is all right. Christ will care for me!"

Quietly I stepped on stage. A sense of profound inner calm and quiet control enfolded my spirit. The presentation was made without pause. The message came across clearly and poignantly. All was well. Thank You, Father!

Several months passed. Then the film producer asked me to set a date for the mountain segment. Because of my life-long experience outdoors, and in the high country, it was felt I would be able to pick the most appropriate time. I agreed to do so only if I was allowed to be myself in this part of the picture. There were to be no more make-up men, no more sound men, no more staged scenes. It was to be a glimpse into my life of handling a sheep dog while caring for a flock in a mountain setting of natural splendor.

The producer agreed to this. They would engage the services of a sheep rancher with a large flock high above timber line in the Rocky Mountains. A champion sheep dog from Texas would be brought in to work with me. Part of the film crew would come from Colorado, part of them from Texas, while Ursula and I would come from California. The logistics of getting us all together at one time in one spot at the crest of the Rockies was rather formidable, especially on the two specific days in the fall I had chosen.

To my dismay, unusually heavy rains began to fall earlier that month in the region chosen for our filming. In fact, the downpours intensified as our shooting date approached. TV reports showed massive devastation around Silverton and Durango. Roads were washed out.

Huge mud and rock slides swept down off the slopes. Mountain trails were becoming impassable. The weather was socked in solid.

The day Ursula and I flew into Mountrose, a small community nearby, there was solid overcast. Sheets of rain fell from the dark clouds. Only two advance men from the entire crew had been able to get in. When they met us they were filled with gloom and doom. The filming would be a fiasco!

After a poor supper I excused myself and went out for a quiet walk alone. It would be a solitary interlude for prayer. Just at dusk a brilliant, scarlet streak of sunset creased the western horizon. In ecstasy I took it as a sign from my Father: "Tomorrow will be a fine day!"

When I shared this conviction with the other men they were less than convinced. In fact, they were decidedly skeptical, especially since it poured rain as we turned in for the night. But my confidence was in Christ, not in the overwhelming circumstances around me.

Ursula and I awoke before dawn. We dressed and went to meet the rest of the crew. No one was around. We waited and waited! Finally, one by one, men began to straggle in after an almost sleepless night. In remarkable ways the road crews had cleared away the rock and mud slides. All the vehicles had gotten through!

Just at that point the tough sheep rancher showed up with his outfit and declared boldly he was sure he could get us up onto the range with our four-wheel drive jeeps. So we were off in high hopes, though the sky was still overcast.

Hour after hour the valiant vehicles growled and clawed their way up the almost impassable mountain trails. In places soil and gravel were all washed away and we bumped and groaned over rough bedrock.

Ursula was flung from side to side in our gallant little vehicle. She leaned over and whispered to me, "Honey,

I'm afraid I may be ruptured by this rough ride!" Our driver had overheard her remark but misunderstood it."Oh, Mrs. Keller," he chimed in. "What better place to be 'raptured' from, than high in these mountains!" We all laughed so loud and hard I thought he might drive us over the cliff edge.

By eleven o'clock we broke out above timber line. Just then the clouds began to dissolve. The blue sky appeared in broken patches. Then I spotted the sheep high on a nearby ridge at about 12,000 feet altitude.

Promptly I assembled all the crew. I told them in plain, blunt language, "Men, we will only have about three hours of favorable conditions before the clouds close in on us. So shoot, shoot, shoot! There is only today to do the job!"

To my unbounded delight the little border collie took to me at once. She responded to my commands and enfolded the sheep with incredible energy. It was as if we had worked together for years.

As the day progressed the sky grew brighter. The mountain vegetation sparkled from the abundant moisture glistening on every leaf and blade of grass. The streams flowed full and all the rock slopes were bathed in lovely light. Filming conditions could not have been more ideal. It was a superb setting!

The film crew worked with intensity. They never spared themselves to capture every aspect of this wondrous upland world. They were filming a man and a dog at home on the range, working a flock with ease and expertise. Within three hours we had all the footage needed to complete the film. I was exuberant and so was the entire crew.

Gathering them all around me at 3:00 o'clock I warned them solemnly. "Men, we got what we came to film. Our Father has been so gracious and kind to us. Now, I urge you all to get down off this mountain before dark settles in. It will begin to rain again. The trails will become impassable. Let's go!"

Without delay they all complied with my instructions. We all got back down to the little frontier town of Silverton just as darkness descended. Weary, yet jubilant with our success, we staggered into a small cafe to try to find some food. In the scramble to get to the sheep, lunches had been forgotten, so most of us were famished.

As we entered the building it began to pour rain again. Nor did the storms relent in that region for the next ten days. But our work was done! A superb film that has blessed thousands of viewers was produced. And once again in His own magnificent manner, our Father had honored the simple faith invested in Him. How dear He is!

Chapter 14

Cars, Trucks and Travel

Anyone who lives in the great expanses of western North America is bound to depend on motor vehicles for long distance transportation. Since the Second World War, a remarkable network of fine highways has been built all across the mountains, plains, valleys and deserts of the tumbled western regions.

Those of us who live in this realm of soaring mountain peaks, rushing rivers and dry deserts have to face the challenges of driving through burning summer heat as well as treacherous winter weather. Ice, snow, sleet and dense fog are all part of the pageantry of life in the west.

To cope with these conditions year after year with assurance means owning and driving motor vehicles which are sturdy and reliable. This poses no great challenge for people who are by natural inclination mechanical in make up and who have a natural affinity for engines or other automotive devices.

Not all of us are skilled in this way. I am a person who is somewhat baffled by the complexity of human engineering. I lack the inborn instinct to grasp how motors are designed or electrical circuits are laid out. Still, I have acquired sufficient experience in handling vehicles that I know special care must be given to their maintenance and great skill should be applied to their operation. So across the years, the cars and trucks I have owned not only provided remarkable services over long spans of time, but they also carried me safely through treacherous traffic and dangerous weather conditions.

A large part of this is caused by my direct dependence on my Father to care for us while we are on the road. I have been acutely aware of His presence in our travels.

It is my implicit conviction that it is just as essential to trust Christ to guide us in the choice of a car or truck to drive as it is in the work we undertake for Him. His wisdom, His knowledge, His guidance in such matters can be sought here as surely as in any other area of life.

It has been my personal experience that in so doing we do not make serious mistakes. We are not stuck with "lemons." We do not end up with "a bucket of bolts" that not only endangers our lives but costs thousands of dollars to repair and keep running on the road.

For us a car or truck is much more than merely a convenience. It is an essential tool required to help accomplish the Master's business. It is the means of transportation required to take us to Bible study sessions at any season of the year under any sort of driving conditions. It is needed to haul our own personal effects and working materials to any place God our Father has a job for us to do. It is the least expensive and by far the most efficient way to accomplish my responsibilities to Him and His people.

Across more than fifty years of driving over a million miles, I have never had a major accident—though I have been spared again and again from very close calls. There have been tense moments when other vehicles around me were in the ditch or in smash-ups, but we were spared from danger. This is not because of "luck," as the world calls it, but because of my Father's constant care for us, and His guardian angels around us.

Rarely if ever do we set out on a long distance drive that we do not bow our heads in simple prayer to request that we be spared from accidents on the road or mechanical failure along the way. The result is that we have had thousands and thousands of hours of trouble-free travel even under the worst weather conditions.

Just two weeks ago I had to make a 1300-mile trip from British Columbia down to Southern California. Early winter weather had moved into the Northwest. Deep snow already lay on the mountain ranges. Dense fog filled the low-lying areas. Black ice was starting to sheath stretches of the higher level highways.

All across Oregon heavy fog enveloped the road. All the way from Portland to the foothills of Mount Shasta I never saw blue sky. The heavy transports and thundering traffic roared along in the dense overcast. Finally I climbed up to the higher elevations. There treacherous black ice sheathed the pavement. Vehicles had skidded into the deep ditches on every side. Yet I passed through in peace. It was with a humble spirit and profound gratitude to my Father that I saw the sun again as it shone clearly over the clouds and bathed Shasta in glorious light.

Later that same day, dense fog again settled into the San Joachin Valley. There it is known as the dangerous "tulle fog." For nearly another 200 miles I traveled through its clinging dampness. It was with unbounded joy that at last I felt the gentle western sun of the south coast envelop me in its warmth.

At such times one travels in trust. There is an acute sense of Christ's companionship in the vehicle. Audibly, without shame or embarrassment, I commune with Him. I ask Him for clarity of mind, swiftness of reflexes, quietness of spirit and strength to withstand the strain of long distance driving. Nor does He deny such requests. Many are those who have been truly astonished at the distances we covered in safety and ease, even under the most adverse driving conditions.

Amid all this I am acutely aware that He has provided His own guardian angels to protect His child on the crowded highways of life. Thank You, Father!

There have been rare occasions when there was a minor malfunction in the car or truck. As with driving, even so, then, we trust our Father for assistance in the situation. There are those who scoff at such a notion, so I relate a couple of instances here to show how He can be trusted for help even amid the complexity of our twentieth century technology.

One evening in mid-winter, just at dusk, we set out for a weekly Bible study I conducted in a small town seventy miles away. When I went to turn on the headlights they simply refused to function in low beam. The only way we could get any light for the trip was to drive with high beams, and then only if I held the lever in place with my left hand. It was too late to phone ahead and tell the class I could not come. So I told Ursula we would have to push on and drive the whole distance while I held the light switch in position.

When we arrived at the class I called on all the men, some of whom were expert mechanics, to have a look at the car to see if they could correct the fault. Everyone concluded that the complicated mechanism in the steering column had broken down. The entire assembly would have to be replaced to remedy the damage.

That really was of little consolation in the middle of the night, with all garages closed and us seventy miles from home. What to do? Friends offered to let us sleep at their home. But I chose, instead, to seek our Father's help.

Ursula and I got in the car quietly. We bowed our hearts and heads in simple confidence, asking for divine assistance in our dilemma. Then in calm assurance I switched the headlights on. They functioned perfectly in low beam. We drove home in perfect safety. Nor did the lights ever again malfunction as long as we owned that car. Some will sneer in derision. We, on the other hand, delight in our Father's provision for us.

On another occasion we were driving down the coastal highway in a brutal winter storm. High winds were driving the surf against the shore in foaming breakers. Deluges of rain streamed from the heavy clouds. The windshield wipers on the truck had to work furiously not only to clear the torrent of water that ran down across the windshield but also to buck the pressure of the gusting winds against them.

At best, visibility was very limited. I could scarcely see through the gloom to drive when suddenly the wipers simply stopped dead. It was impossible to go on. So I pulled off to the side of the road. Try as I might, I could do nothing to start the wipers again.

Finally a local man in an old pick-up truck stopped to see if he could help. I told him our trouble. He was sorry to tell me that there was no garage on this remote stretch of the coastline for about twenty-three miles. And he knew nothing about repairing electrical wipers. I thanked him for his trouble, then he was on his way.

I climbed back into the driver's seat, remarking to Ursula, "Only our Father can help us here!" So without fanfare or facetious pretense of any sort we gently entreated our Father God to intervene on our behalf. It was a simple prayer of implicit trust in Him.

Quietly I switched on the motor, then in calm confidence I turned on the wipers. They worked perfectly for the rest of the trip. Nor did they ever malfunction again. Overwhelming gratitude sprang up within us.

Perhaps the reader will wonder why I bother to recount such events. It is not to try to impress people with our unusual faith, simple as it is. Rather, my desire is to demonstrate how, even in this complex mechanical age, our Father can be counted on to care for us in wondrous ways. He is everywhere present and active in the affairs of those who will trust Him fully.

There are occasions on which skeptics, cynics and worldly wise men challenge me to prove God even exists. My reply to them, given without arrogance or condescension, is simply to say, "Look at my life." In a hundred tiny details He cares for me in wondrous ways. It is not the great, sensational, spectacular displays of His divine power that impress me. Rather, it is in the minute details of His daily care and constant companionship that I discover the endearing reality of His eternal person.

Therein lies the glory of God, my Father. Here is the endearing, warm companionship of Christ. In this way one walks in the counsel and quiet guidance of God's Gracious Spirit. If He can provide for sparrows and lillies and grass in the meadow, He can also care for me—and He does! Yes, even amid all the technology of the twentieth century.

Often the manner in which He does this is through the generous hearts and skilled hands of His other dear children. Almost everywhere He has led me, there have been big-hearted men who gladly offered to tune up my engines or make minor repairs at little or no cost. I sense somehow they felt this was one way they could serve as Good Samaritans. But more than that, it was one way in which they helped to achieve God's gracious work in the world. So in it there was a double blessing for all of us.

Even in the purchase of vehicles, I have carefully sought my Father's guidance, for, with my limited knowledge, serious errors could be made. A case in point was the purchase of a small compact car for Ursula.

She had a handsome but very large 1977 Cutlass Supreme. It was the last of the line of big cars built in the '70s. On our narrow, steep, winding roads it was not a suitable vehicle for her to handle. Though old, it was in mint condition. We decided to ask $4,000.00 for it on a trade, this being a fair and conservative value.

When we had been directed to the exact car best suited to her needs, the car dealer asked what she had to trade. We told him it was the Olds Cutlass Supreme, for which we wanted $4,000.00.

He took the car for a test drive. He agreed it was in excellent condition, with low mileage and fine performance. However, he insisted, the "blue book" value was only $2,500.00 and that was all he would allow us.

We declined his offer, stating he should test drive it again while we went across the street for lunch. When we came back we felt sure he would accept our proposal, because this would give us time to pray.

When we returned the manager called us into his office. He said they had reconsidered and would in fact give Ursula $4,000.00 for her car. My part was simply to pay $100.00 to have it transferred, which I was glad to do.

To our amusement the manager, when told by Ursula that we had been praying about the deal, added that he, too, had been doing the same. It sounded plausible but seemed highly unlikely.

We drove home in the new car in joyous delight. Late that night the phone rang. It was a family we had not seen for several years. They asked if in fact we had traded in our Olds Cutlass Supreme that day. We assured them we had. Then they told us they had purchased the car that afternoon from the dealer.

In happy enthusiasm they recounted how exactly at noon, while we were having lunch, they had phoned this dealer and asked him if he happened to have a 1977 Olds Cutlass Supreme for sale. They had driven one for years, loved it so well they wanted another, but with low mileage.

There our car stood, waiting for them, all prepared in advance by our Father to meet the needs of two families who trusted Him even in car buying and selling. They were elated and so were we!

Chapter 15

The Joy of a Far-Flung Family

Some of us, under the providential arrangement of The Most High, have fewer family members than others by natural birth. For example, in my home I was the only child who survived. My twin brothers both succumbed at birth. So I was bereft of any siblings. Both of my parents passed on to their eternal home with Christ at a fairly early age by modern measurement. In turn, I had only two children. The end result was that there are far fewer people in my immediate family circle than might otherwise be the case.

Still in His gentle, gracious, sympathetic way our Father has more than made up for this deficiency through the dear people He has brought into my life. I was only twenty-two years old when my Dad died. He had been my unabashed boyhood hero. The caliber of his character, his amazing accomplishments, the serene strength of his close walk with Christ left an indelible imprint on my boyhood years.

When he died suddenly at the age of fifty-four I felt really quite forlorn and lonely—especially since I was thousands of miles away from home in a country which was still strange and unfamiliar to a foreign-born youth. In gentle, tender and caring ways, my Father arranged for other strong, sturdy men, sure in their faith, to fill the void in my life. For me they became like surrogate dads who could provide the guidance, wisdom and example I needed so desperately.

Several of these were stalwart missionaries, who literally laid down their lives for the remote and far-flung loggers, fishermen and settlers of Canada's tough west coast. Those hardy, courageous men are still among my dearest friends. Their affection, their prayers are an ongoing benediction to this day.

Again and again there has swept over my spirit an acute awareness that these men were interceding for me in the hour of extremity. Unexpected phone calls, the occasional letter in the mail, a personal visit now and then—all are precious reminders that they care, they think about me, they are petitioning Christ on my behalf. Such living assurance is precious indeed! It reminds me often that my Father in His noble way more than makes up for any family loss suffered.

In precisely the same way rich provision has been made to supply me with loving, gracious women who have in truth been as dear as any mother. One of these, who took me into her home and into her heart when I was a strong-willed wayward young man, has since gone to glory. But a portion of the credit for my redemption from ruin was the great-hearted generosity of this dear widow. Amid her own poverty and loneliness she reached out to draw me gently back into the family of God.

Much the same was true for other white-haired, sweet-spirited women who cared enough to "adopt" someone as tough and rough as I was. And down across the long years of my adventurous life they have followed my progress with incredible fidelity and unflinching love.

None of these have been accidental encounters. Rather, they are the rare and beautiful arrangements made by my Father to enrich and enlarge my earthly family. For I do, in fact, feel just as great an attachment to them as to my natural birth parents—perhaps even more so, for the simple reason that I am humbled and astonished to realize they care so deeply despite all my shortcomings. Across the years, across the long miles that separate us, across the great gaps of time when we seldom see each other, their warmth and affection remain steadfast.

Down the long pilgrimage of my path, special people of quiet courage and enormous goodwill have drawn me into the gentle embrace of their open hearts and homes. It is no small thing to be accepted with warmth and enduring affection by men and women who once were utter strangers. This sense of "belonging" to a far-flung family fills me with remarkable joy and gratitude. In truth I sense an acute and unique kinship with people whom my Father has chosen to be my surrogate family.

The amazing aspect of all this arrangement is that it does not depend upon natural human ties. It does not rest in bonds of filial relationships. Nor has it been cemented by traditional inheritance of common roots. Quite the opposite! Some of those who are the dearest come from backgrounds totally foreign to mine. Yet it has not diminished our devotion to each other. Such is the wondrous provision made for our mutual support and encouragement in our Father's concern. We have accepted one another without reservation. Therein lies the wonder of it all. Thank You, Father!

When all is said and done, there remains one great central conclusion. It is this: "If we are truly to love the Lord our God with all our spirit, soul and strength, it must be as we find Him in other people!" They will not always be either the most compatible characters nor the most pleasing personalities. But they will be those chosen by Christ to become our far-flung family.

Some of my associates are astonished at the sorts of individuals who have become dear to me. They are amazed that often my friends come from the "wrong side of the tracks." They are surprised that I do not deliberately cultivate the company of so-called "successful" or influential people. Christ was accused of being a friend to publicans and sinners. Why should I be different, if I own His family name?

The love, affection and enduring faithfulness, which a former generation has shown to me, I, in turn, have endeavored to pass on to others younger than myself. As Jesus Himself put it so simply, "Freely you have received, so freely give of yourself to others." This is an integral part of finding abundant joy and deep satisfaction in our wider family scattered across the continent wherever our Father has led us to serve Him.

Just as I had been "adopted," as it were, by those much older than myself, so for my part a sincere effort has been made to adopt others into my far-flung family. Or perhaps it might be more proper to say they have adopted me and Ursula. At least they well-nigh regard us with the warm winsomeness of those who are parents and guardians.

This has come about with family after family, not by some special strategy or prearranged plan, but simply by sensing it was our Father's beautiful desire for both of us. By the manner in which our paths crossed; our concerns for each other were ignited. Our association deepened with mutual benefit and encouragement for all concerned. This has been a beautiful benediction.

It is a unique pleasure and rare privilege to feel that one is a member of such an association. This sort of attachment is much more profound than the usual loose companionship of a church group. It far transcends the sort of casual fellowship often cultivated in clubs, societies or growth groups.

The family ties I am here referring to have to do with a depth of devotion equal to and exceeding that of a regular family. The bond is a deep, enduring concern for the welfare of the others. So much so that we are not ashamed to weep with those who weep, to relish laughing with those who laugh, to rejoice with those who are led gently in the paths of peace by our Father.

Ever since we were married our Father has enriched and expanded our lives with the simple, lovely, yet joyous provision of a wider family made up of young couples. In ways beyond understanding they would be drawn to us and we to them in bonds of deep affection and loving loyalty.

The first such couple I recall so clearly had come to Hawaii in a spirit of adventure. There they met and courted, much of the time while attending the Bible classes I taught in Waikiki. We became very fond of each other. I remember so vividly helping them move into their first home with all the fun and gaiety that attends such an adventure.

The bride was a lovely girl of superb character—one of those rare and beautiful ladies in whom Christ lived with manifest serenity and repose. Each time one met her it was to be enriched and uplifted by her sweet and gentle spirit.

Little did we realize, or ever dream, that her call "home" to be with Christ would come so soon and so early in life. She was stricken with a most virulent form of cancer. Her magnificent young life was cut short. But she was fully prepared for her greater glory. Our loss was heaven's gain. How she was missed by those of us who knew and loved her with admiration and esteem.

In Australia our Father in His tender concern for our companionship gave us another dear pair of young people to lighten our days and cheer our spirits. They had a beautiful home in Canberra. He held an important post in the government. Both of them were gracious, cordial people who wholeheartedly opened their hearts and their home to us. We had hilarious times together.

Only one dark cloud overshadowed their lives. They were childless. Every endeavor made to bear children had proved fruitless. Because the young lady had been a fully qualified radiologist, it was thought perhaps she had been inadvertently exposed to excessive radiation that made it impossible to conceive.

One day, in a quiet but very confidential conversation with them about this concern, I shared an old homespun secret with them. If they were both to take substantial doses of extra iodine in their diet they might well be surprised. This they calmly agreed to do. Combining this simple remedy with prayer and quiet trust in our Father, we waited quietly to see what He would do.

It was not long until they sent us an ecstatic letter of great joy. Julie was expecting their first child. The infant was delivered without difficulty and became the forerunner of several siblings. Little wonder we were considered surrogate grandparents.

When we returned to Canada we were again drawn into a gentle relationship of goodwill and mutual affection with young couples who were courting and would soon be married. It was not that we saw them frequently, but rather a case where they knew assuredly we cared for them deeply and prayed fervently for their future under our Father's care.

Much to my unbounded delight two of these dear couples committed themselves fully to overseas missionary endeavor.

One pair eventually found their way to Kenya where in a sense I felt they were playing the role which I had longed to fill as a younger man, but could not carry out because of my inability to live in the tropics. The other couple first served in establishing a vigorous church in a tough Canadian community, then later went to serve in Zaire and Belgium.

When we moved down to California our Father again was pleased to broaden the bounds of our family. In His inimitable compassion and gracious mercy He never ever left us bereft of younger people to brighten our days. For it is young people with their energy, their enthusiasm, their vigor, their fun, their escapades of daring adventure who inject an exciting dimension into life.

In Santa Barbara a dear young couple were drawn into the orbit of our affections in such a way that they are in very truth like children to us. The beauty of this companionship lies in the simple fact that we have fully accepted each other without reservation or restrictions. We simply do not put undue demands upon each other. There is no expectation of perfection or utter infallibility in each other. We find enormous goodwill, fun, delight and quiet contentment in each other's company.

Because neither one of these precious people comes from a Christian home, they look upon us as second parents in the realm of their spiritual growth. And indeed it has been wonderful to watch the gradual maturity of their relationship with Christ. Not only has this been a keen inspiration to us but a magnificent benediction to their three splendid sons now growing into sturdy manhood.

Another delightful couple drawn into our lives by the bonds of God's grace now serve a thriving community church in the city. They have stood steadfast in that place where most people would long ago have given up in despair.

Our Father is honoring their fortitude and faith. He has seen the travail of their souls in that tough spot. Not only is He bringing them out of the fires of adversity as refined gold, but also He is calling out a special people in that place to be His beautiful bride. For us it is a special honor to be their friends and part of their family! Thank You, Father!

Chapter 16

Touching Both Prosperous and Poor

There is no question at all that it was our Father's arrangement for us to spend some of our years in Santa Barbara, California. It is often assumed by the general public that Southern California with its balmy climate, beautiful beaches, breath-taking scenery, and abundance of fruit and flowers is a part of paradise. Some of the locals even refer to it as "our bit of heaven." One wit went so far as to comment, *"Who cares about going to glory when they can live in California?"*

Still there is another side to all this splendor. It is the aspect often not well understood by those who have never lived there. Despite its apparent affluence, despite its flamboyant life style, despite all the exciting stimulation of its aggressive society, it stands as one of the truly neediest mission fields in all the world.

I was to discover this first hand soon after we moved there. Nor has the burden of attempting to touch, lift and redeem both prosperous and poor ever left me since we arrived. Even though this region of the country has produced more than its share of great churches, stirring preachers and world-renowned radio and television broadcasts of the gospel, it still remains one of the tough, tough mission fields of the world. This is especially true if one desires to make a personal impact upon the lives of people who reside here, work here and call California home.

It is not enough in this corrupt culture to merely astound the masses with superb showmanship in religious endeavors. If one is to be true to Christ there comes the acute awareness that a man or woman who truly loves Him will need to get beneath the glitter and glamor to touch people in their poverty or prosperity.

To truly be Christ's follower here was to encounter people from both extremes of the social spectrum. I had been invited to start Bible studies in the city. Most of those who came initially were very wealthy people. Sometimes the study sessions were held in the local club houses. Here the rich, the sophisticated, the upper crust of the community assembled to hear God's Word.

It never ceased to astonish me how the very well-to-do individuals were constantly preoccupied with their own personal security. By this I do not just mean safety, but rather the acquisition and possession of more and more property, assets and/or investments of one kind or another to shelter them against any possible misfortune. Being so inordinantly wealthy they impressed me as being terribly poor in spirit, shriveled in soul, blighted by their largesse which was like a weighted millstone about their necks.

What saddened me even more as we came to know these people privately was their rigid reluctance to part with their possessions for the benefit of the poor. Often it seemed the more wealth a person acquired, the more tenanciously they clung to what they owned. It was not uncommon to have multimillionaires sit on the couch beside me in our humble home adamantly refuse to share some of their riches with the needy. These people weighed heavily on my spirit. And even though I would implore them to experience the joy and delight of sharing something with the poor and destitute, they preferred to turn a deaf ear.

As time went on I sometimes remarked that "God called Mother Teresa to minister to the poorest of the poor, and He called me to minister to the richest of the rich." And of the two opposite segments of society, it seemed that as of old it could truly be said, "It is harder for the rich to enter into the Kingdom of Heaven, than it is for a camel to pass through the eye of a needle." The poor, it seemed, were pleased and eager to receive the Good News of our Father's Love.

Because transients who drifted up and down the coast found sunshine, warmth and some respite from harsh winter weather in this lovely spot by the sea, they congregated here in fairly large numbers. They would sleep in the thickets along the roads; they sometimes huddled in the sandy coves beneath the sea cliffs; or they took refuge in any culvert or vacant building that offered shelter from rain or wind.

It grieved me deeply to see the drifters who lived in such abject poverty and hopelessness. Among them were young women, even some with tiny children. In harsh weather they would paw through the trash containers placed in public places hoping to find fragments of food to assuage their grim hunger pangs.

All this seemed a painful paradox in an affluent community where people at the other end of the social spectrum lived in grand opulence. It reminded me forcefully of the deeply moving story the Master told of the rich man who banqueted in luxury. Outside his door a poor beggar lay on the steps with only stray dogs to lick his wounds and bring him solace.

Many of the wealthy people in the community found the poor and destitute to be an irritation and acute embarrassment. They did not want these people on their doorsteps nor on their lovely streets. They passed all sorts of local by-laws to keep them on the move, to send them on their way, to expel them from the environs of the town.

Only those with generous hearts of compassion and genuine sympathy for these tragic people attempted to alleviate the distress of the poor. Amongst them were social workers, the stalwart Salvation Army citadel, and a local Christian Rescue Mission which had been active for years.

It was the Rescue Mission that drew our greatest interest and support. In large part this was because of the steadfast efforts made in that humble place not only to feed and house the poor, but also to bring them into a personal encounter with the Living Christ.

Both Ursula and I believed that the Rescue Mission touched more lives for the Master in any given year than even the largest churches in town. A dear, devoted couple of enormous experience and godly wisdom supervised the work. To their unbounded credit it can be said that literally hundreds of destitute men were brought into a new life of decency and integrity through their efforts. Of course, many Christians in the community contributed to this project, helping to make it a living monument to our Father's love.

During the time of our residence in the city, the need for more accommodation and better facilities for the mission became acute. We began a search to find a suitable site where a new mission could be built. It was felt accommodation should be provided for both men and women who drifted into town.

Try as they might, the board of directors was blocked again and again in their endeavors to relocate. Local businessmen, shop keepers, residents and petty politicians of one sort or another opposed the idea vehemently. They were afraid somehow that such a facility would deprecate the reputation of the town and depreciate property values.

Instead of lending full-hearted support to such a project, community leaders actually opposed it. As if to hand the mission a sop of bitter herbs to mitigate their suffering in this painful enterprise, the city council offered them a site at an outrageous price.

It was at this juncture that The Gracious Spirit of God impressed upon my spirit that we should take rather drastic steps to help in securing a new site for the mission. There come times in life when it is no longer good enough to sit around and just commiserate with others doing royal battle for God in our sordid society. If His work is going to be done, it demands that we make substantial personal sacrifices to see our Father's purposes carried through to completion. This was one of those times.

Actually, since the Rescue Mission provides such yeoman service to the entire community, the city should have provided a suitable site free of charge—or, at least at a nominal charge of a dollar a year. This they adamantly refused to do. So things came to a deadlock with the mission in no position to pay such a high price for a place to build new facilities.

After earnest prayer and quiet communion with Christ, it became clear to Ursula and me that we should offer our home as an outright gift to secure funds for the mission. There came to me the quiet assurance that our Father in His generous way could easily provide us with another place to live if we we were willing to part with this home.

I called up a dear friend who had been more or less the original founder of the work, as well as the devoted director. Both he and the supervisor were invited to our home for a chat. That afternoon, with the warm sun enfolding the coast in its embrace, we gave our home away to be used to help others in dire need. It was a moment in time we would not forget. It was the right and appropriate thing to do without fanfare or display.

Proceeds from the sale of our home would serve as a catalyst to bring about stirring changes. Others would catch a vision of what could be achieved for God. The work would go on!

The end result has been the erection of a beautiful building complex that is an enormous asset to the entire community. The mayor was bold enough to declare one whole month "Santa Barbara Rescue Mission Month." There is abroad amongst the hotel and motel owners a new awareness that the Rescue Mission is performing a noble service for the overall benefit of all citizens. Instead of antagonism, there is abroad an attitude of approval for what has been accomplished.

Best of all has been the benefit coming to the poor and destitute who drift into this lovely seaside town. Here they can meet the Master. Here they can have their lives changed and find new hope for the future. Here they can be trained in a new trade to go out and serve others with dignity.

In all this progress our Father looks on and is pleased. He is cheered and consoled by the sterling sacrifices made by His children to seek the lost and lift up the downtrodden. In this way His love, compassion and generosity are given to those in need.

The interlude of our sojourn by the sea was now drawing to a close. My fond personal hope had been that we could live in Santa Barbara for the rest of my days. It was not to be. My Father had fresh work for me to do in the north. At the time its exact nature and extent were unknown. Still this did not dismay me. In my gentle walk with Christ I had learned that He would prepare a new place for us. He would make clear the fresh responsibilities entrusted to me and He would provide the energy and endurance of His own person to accomplish His purposes through us. All was well!

Meanwhile, a deep, profound and very precious upwelling of gratitude flowed to my Father for all the generous bounties bestowed upon us in this lovely city. Here my health and vitality had been restored to me in wondrous ways without human aid. Here He had enabled me to write and compile some fifteen books. Several of these were magnificent volumes illustrated with my own photographs, a life-long dream come to fruition. Here He allowed me to teach many, many classes with courage and concern for the entire community. Because of my boldness many called me "The Prophet," a title I was not ashamed to bear.

A surprising number of the books became best sellers. The proceeds from them were passed on to the poor, destitute and underprivileged of the earth. In any way it was possible, we tried to touch lives far beyond our shores. If I could not go myself, at least in this way I could help dispel the darkness, despair and degradation in which others groped for hope.

That hope was in Christ and we were His bearers of great Good News to all men everywhere. What an honor! Thank You, Father!

Chapter 17

Chalet Sunshine

As the time drew near for us to leave California it became very clear that we should return to Canada. The question was just where should we reside? I had lived on Vancouver Island with its gentle maritime climate; up in the interior Okanagan region with its lovely lakes and rugged mountains; as well as out on the rolling prairies of Alberta. This is an enormous region. Exactly where did our Father want us to work?

After weeks of explicit prayer we were clearly convinced that our place was to be found in the high dry mountain terrain of British Columbia's interior. I had no doubt our Father had prepared a place for us. My job was to find it in forthright faith, trusting Him quietly to lead me to it.

Because Ursula was afflicted with tendonitis in her arms, we knew it would be wise to live in a dry region where she could recover. Also, the house needed to be only modest in size with large cheerful windows to fill it with sunshine and warmth to aid her condition.

I left Santa Barbara before dawn, and two days later pulled into the driveway of Harvie's home. He was a longtime friend with whom I had hiked many a mountain trail. I slept like a log after such a long drive. The next morning

I met an agent who had three homes to show me high up in the hills in a lovely location beside a beautiful golf course.

When I walked into the third home, a brand new cedar chalet with huge windows overlooking the greens and soaring mountains beyond, I knew I had found the place. It had been built with enormous care. No expense had been spared to make it a lovely retirement home. Then the wealthy family who owned it had suddenly faced serious financial reverses. They needed to recoup their losses. The agent said they would sell it to me for two thirds of its cost of construction.

By 10:30 that morning I had found the place of our Father's appointment. A great peace and quiet contentment enfolded my spirit. All was well! When, a few weeks later, Ursula stepped into its sun-splashed interior she was ecstatic. Immediately she called the home "Chalet Sunshine." There her health would be restored, and there we would fulfill the precise purposes for which our Father had called us back to this rugged region.

The first of these responsibilities was to become closely, painfully, lovingly involved with families who faced terminal illnesses. Little did I dream that this would include some of my dearest friends. Harvie himself, who had come to know and love Christ through my classes years before, would become one of my fondest friends, then suddenly be stricken with massive cancer of the brain.

It was to be a formidable ordeal. And as he and his brave little wife Marie walked through the valley of the shadow of death, we, too, with tears, anguish and pain walked by their side. It is no easy thing to see a great, rugged, stalwart man who could climb any mountain trail with ease, succumb to the cruel ravages of this dread disease.

We were high on a snow-shrouded slope one winter day when I first noticed Harvie was losing his agility and coordination. I had to help him across some steep, ice-sheathed rock ledges, and I wondered to myself what was wrong. His condition deteriorated rapidly. Within about seven months he had wasted away to a mere skeleton of bone and sinew.

He was taken from us. There was enormous sorrow in his going for he was dearly beloved, closer to me than any brother of blood or birth could ever be. Again and again Marie remarked, "Only our Father knew how much we would need you here to stand by us in this anguish. That's why He brought you back."

Over a period of roughly three years our lives would be intertwined with some thirty different families who faced the scourge of disease, death and disaster. In very truth and in living, wrenching reality, we were tasting death with others. We were being torn by the tormenting, burning questions which have wrung such heart cries from the human family across the centuries.

> Why so much pain?
> Why such grievous separation?
> Why sorrow upon sorrow?
> Why the deep despair and awesome anguish?

All of this was in fact to be partakers of Christ's own sufferings for His people. Here there was an intimate and intense identification with Him in His sorrow. No wonder He is called "The Man of Sorrows, the One acquainted with grief"—not only His own, but ours as well.

Out of this crucible of pressure and pain and pathos, clear, concise answers began to come to me about God's purposes in death. Gradually as I sought the solace of His spirit and sensed the presence of His person amid the anguish of it all, clear and specific reasons were revealed to me for the pain of parting. These I decided to record in the book I wrote at the time entitled *Sky Edge*.

In simple, yet profound parables drawn from the rugged mountain realm around us I could understand something of the mystery of suffering. These were shared with the reader, and I have been encouraged to hear how our Father uses those insights to lift the load and heal the spirits of those who face death.

No, it was not by accident or happenstance that we were led back to those rugged mountain ranges. Our Father had a mission of healing, of help, of new hope for us to bring in mercy and love and gentle kindness to those in distress. It was not easy, but it was His will!

Then there was another friend. Like Harvie, he, too, was a strong, tough, stalwart fellow who lived in the little lakeside community about five miles below us. One dawn his dear wife called to say her man had been felled with a massive stroke. He lay prostrate in the hospital unable to move or speak.

He had first come to the Bible studies with a rather difficult attitude and ready to argue. Yet in gentle grace and quiet perseverance Christ had drawn him to Himself. He had become a dear friend and across the years strong bonds had been forged between us.

I went down to see him at once. The hospital room seemed so severe, so stark, so dark. His daughter, a mature woman, broken and shattered, bent over him, tears cascading down her cheeks and over his face. Their world seemed so bleak, so black, so foreboding.

Together we prayed earnestly that our Father would have mercy in restoring mobility to this man's inert body. Somehow the assurance came that unlike Harvie, he would not die. God still had some special work for this strong man to do. What could it be? With patient perseverance his wife helped him articulate words again.

Wonder of wonders, strength began to flow again into his great frame. Muscles, tendons, nerves and sinews began to respond to impulses from his brain. For a long time his speech was slurred and words were hard to form. But in amazing, creative energy he discovered he could draw. And his drawings were superb!

A portrait he did of Christ in pen and ink with a charcoal background is one of the most beautiful I have ever seen. At my urging it was framed and hung in their home. This Christmas every card they sent out bore that portrait with the message of Christ's presence in their lives.

My friend was restored. He is strong and sturdy again. Now he does all the artwork for the children's classes in his church. Thank You, Father!

There were other reasons, also unknown to me, that God's call back to Canada came so clearly. One of these was the underground drug scene in the community. It was not the sort of area the average person would even think drug trafficking would take place The quiet little lakeside towns; the fruit orchards flourishing in the sun; the rough cattle ranges dotted with herds of Herefords and Angus hardly seemed the setting for large-scale drug dealing. In fact, it was one of the most active in all of western Canada. And I was to be plunged into the madness of it all in a most unusual manner.

A couple came to one of my lectures one evening. Afterward the man confronted me with a most belligerent attitude. Bluntly he told me he did not like me; he could not agree with what I said; and in short, I simply was not "his cup of tea." I could not help but laugh, and I explained quietly that his attitude did not surprise or shock me.

He seemed astonished. Somehow, God's Spirit overcame his intransigence and later he became one of the most regular and loyal participants in the Bible studies. Subsequently, he and his wife invited Ursula and me to have lunch in their home, a cute cottage perched precariously, high up on a steep hill.

His handsome teenage son was present for the meal. He impressed me as a dear young man. But suddenly, after dunning his dad for a a few dollars, he disappeared. I asked where he was going. Quite nonchalantly the parents informed us he was going down to "The Hole" to procure drugs. He was an addict, a drop-out, and like his older brothers a heartbreak in the home.

After the dad unburdened himself of his anger, frustration and impotence at coping with the curse, I was so moved I offered to meet with the lad. Nothing happened for weeks. Then one day the phone rang. The young man would see me the next morning at 10:30 if I came round to the house. It was mid-winter. Deep snow and ice covered the country.

Gingerly I fought my way up the dangerous road to the home on the hill, my truck clawing its way across the snow and ice. Just as I neared the home I was outraged to find a battered old vehicle deliberately jammed in the driveway to prevent my progress. At great risk I backed all the way down the dangerous hill. Parking the truck at the bottom, I hiked up the long drive. I was not to be put off that easily.

The house literally vibrated with hard rock sounds. I beat on the door, but no one answered. So I began to kick it with my heavy boots until it was about to break down. The alarmed young man rushed up from the basement before I smashed my way in. "Why did you block the drive?" I challenged him with a low growl and piercing eyes. "You picked the wrong man for your little games! I'm coming in!"

He was astonished and taken aback. Without fanfare or polite preliminaries I began to talk to him very forthrightly about the destructive consequences of drug use in his life. Suddenly there were heavy footsteps coming up the stairs. A second tough young man, unkempt and belligerent, came into the room. His eyes smoldered with contempt. He challenged everything I said in open ridicule and defiance.

Finally I stood to my feet. Facing him fearlessly I stated firmly, "It was this young man who asked me to come here and talk to him, not you! I intend to stay. If you interrupt the conversation again I will ask you to leave!"

His whole demeanor suddenly changed. Both young fellows began to listen attentively to what I said. Even more surprising, our Father prevailed by His presence to persuade them to disclose everything to me about the drug trade in the valley. They themselves admitted they were both drug dealers. They knew all the ways and means used to distribute drugs. To my horror they disclosed that even eight-year-old children in school were being victimized. They told me everything!

After a full hour and a half of deep discussion I rose to leave. The tough youth jumped to his feet, stood to attention, then stretched out his hand to me. "Mr. Keller, I apologize for my disorderly conduct! I'm glad you came and talked to us so boldly!" I was astonished.

This incident placed an enormous burden on my spirit. Immediately I set out to try to alert people in the community to the awful peril they faced. With burning concern I shared what I had learned with the people who attended my Bible studies. I took every opportunity given to me to speak about it in churches, though it seemed most Christians in the larger churches only yawned and declared, "Oh dear!" I shared my concern with private citizens wherever I went.

Little by little my endeavors began to ignite a flame of concern among a wide variety of people drawn from various sectors of society. A middle-aged man, delivered from drug addiction himself, offered to go down and "work the 'hole'" to help redeem young people. A mother who herself had gone through agony with two sons hooked on drugs volunteered to go into the elementary schools to warn both teachers and young children of the peril. She was received warmly.

Elderly women came forward, willing to meet with young addicts on the streets and thus become loving, surrogate mothers to the "freaked-out" youths. A service club sponsored an education program designed to reach young people in danger of drugs. Another organization called "Break Away" began to function in helping free the afflicted.

In response to all this my soul was stirred, and my spirit soared in humble gratitude. "Oh, my Father, I thank You for moving upon the lives of Your people! How faithful You are to draw near to us in our distress!"

Chapter 18

Mountain Majesty

Returning to British Columbia brought us back, once more, into intimate contact with the mountains. It is not generally known that "B.C.," as we call it affectionately, is essentially a vast mountain region. Some 98 percent of its rugged terrain is thrust up in gigantic rock ridges. Many of the highest peaks are shrouded in snow most of the year, heavily cloaked with forests along their lower slopes.

In some of the drier inland valleys gray sage-brush, range, or tawny bunch-grass rangelands, supplant the forests. Thousands of lakes, streams and water-courses lace the wild valleys. Here wildlife flourish and here a thin sprinkling of loggers, miners, ranchers, orchardists and other small town residents make their homes. No matter where one resides in B.C., there are mountains in view, hills on the horizon, wild country to be explored. It is such a huge region that all three states of California, Oregon and Washington combined could easily fit within its far-flung boundaries.

Since I am essentially a "son of the wilds," this high mountain realm has always stirred my spirit and nourished my soul with its wild splendor and magnificent majesty. So much space and challenge have nourished me as a man. They have provided much of the inspiration, uplift and energy to be a creative person. For this reason I have always regarded the mountains as a unique and special endowment from my Father. They are a particular part of the planet which has contributed to the rough, tough shaping of my character.

And now in advanced age I again found deep joy, glorious grandeur and bright delight in their company.

It has been well said that "Cain built the first city on earth, and every city since has contributed to the corruption of human society." The basic reason is that in the "man-made, man-controlled" community the presence and power of our Father tend to be constricted within the stone and glass walls of man-made sanctuaries.

On the other hand, His splendor and majesty cannot be so confined in the boundless glory of an open ocean nor in the thrilling grandeur of a great mountain range. Such glorious sweeping spaces with their sublime solitude and stirring vistas can humble a person's proud heart. They can still our souls in the presence of Christ's person. They can supply a more proper perspective to our short and fleeting sojourn on this planet.

Not only do mountain interludes inject a special sort of physical challenge into life with their tough trails and steep slopes, they also enlarge our own spiritual horizons. I say this with great earnestness simply because there is an element of uplift, inspiration and moral stimulation here of unusual proportions. If one is at all sensitive in spirit to the presence of The Most High in His created universe, he will be deeply touched by the high country.

Mountains have their own unique way of humbling a man's haughty heart. Mountains provide an ideal setting in which "to think long thoughts" about the true meaning of life. Mountains can put eternal issues into proper perspective, God's perspective, for us. The wind in the pines, the laughing songs of the streams, the shining snow slopes glistening in the sun, the wild alpine meadows adorned with fields of flowers, the majestic movements of elk, moose, deer, caribou, bears and coyotes are each a part of divine pageantry.

For me as a man it was no small thrill, so late in life, to be allowed once more to roam freely across the mountain ranges. By the time this book appears in print I will have seen seventy summers come and go. Yet in His generous kindness my Father has supplied me with sufficient stamina and bodily energy to still climb rugged slopes and steep snowfields. He has spared my vision to such a degree that without the aid of glasses I can spot a wild sheep at half a mile across a canyon or examine the delicate form of a Flicker's bright feather a few inches away from my face. My pulse still quickens and my blood still courses strongly through my arteries at just the thought of lacing on climbing boots and heading for the high country for a ramble on the ridges.

Such a legacy, so late in life, is no small gift. When a man in the twilight of life's journey still finds enormous delight in the haunting cry of a wolf on a wilderness ridge; when his spirit stirs again at the lonely cry of a loon across a northern lake; when a gleaming grin creases his weather-worn features at the sound of Bighorn Rams in battle, or the rattle of Elk antlers caught up in the rutting struggle for supremacy, that man is drinking deeply from fountains of invigoration known to very few.

Little did I ever dream that so late in my humble pilgrimage along the winding ways of an adventuresome life, my Father would endow my days with so much joy. There in the mountains He supplied the gentle solace and quiet healing needed for my anguished spirit, so pained, so strained by the loss of my dearest friend, Harvie. Together we had shared so many hikes. We had climbed so many slopes in close company, and we had relished so many hearty laughs. We had spent so many still moments basking in each other's friendship. Only the mountains could mend the rending of my soul. And they did, in gentle healing ways.

As the years advance it is imperative that a person, if he is to retain some of the enthusiasm of youth, should accept new challenges. One cannot continually look back to reflect on the past—even though the past is packed full of precious memories. Such memories are a special benefit and bounty from our Father. Still there remains the compelling initiative which can come only from tackling a new adventure, taking on a fresh task, matching one's mind and muscles and spirit to a compelling challenge.

It takes courage to do this. It means running risks. Sometimes it calls for doing the thing you fear most. You cannot always play it safe and snug. One has to step out of the comfortable circle of ease and safety to find the rush and flush of new life forces surging strongly through one's days.

This I was prepared to tackle. So my wanderings across the northern mountains took me into all sorts of thrilling terrain. I explored new trails in the Selkirk Mountains of B.C. I roamed the giant snow-draped ranges of the Rockies in British Columbia and Alberta. My field trips led deep into Montana and even out across the rolling prairies to the Cypress Hills in Saskatchewan. The wide new vistas, the great brooding spaces, the magnificent array of wildlife enlivened me just as much as when I had first come west as a young man some fifty years before.

Now as then I refused to be constrained or tied down by danger. I was ready to tackle any trail, to explore any new ridge, to approach any wild animal, be it a bull moose, a bear or a wolf. Life was for living. The days were made for adventure. The nights were to be filled with firelight, starlight and the mellow memories of magic moments in the mountains. All this was heady stuff. It did not make for boredom or ennui. Thank You, Father! Life is still exciting!

A dynamic part of these high country hikes and long cross-country excursions was the rekindled enthusiasm for outdoor photography. I came home with magnificent photographs to share with Ursula and others who visited in our home. To her great credit, "Cheri," my pet name for Ursula, was gracious enough to share me with the wild places, to send me off in good cheer to meet the unknown challenges of "the mountain man."

Of these, only two little interludes will be retold here to give the reader some idea of the exhilaration mountain memories can inject into a man's experience. Such events, of course, provide more than just memories; at the time they call forth courage, self-discipline, high energy output and intense mental concentration. On top of all this there is exhilarating inspiration, co-mingled with superb spiritual satisfaction.

It was an early spring day. The deep winter snow still clung to the higher crags and cornices. Three mountain goats had been compelled to find forage on the rugged outcrops and lower ledges lying at the base of a magnificent mountain. Cool air flowed down the remote slope from the snow pack above. So conditions were ideal to begin a hard climb in order to get within camera range. I chose not to use a long lens, preferring to have the thrill of stalking the wild ones with my old hunting skills.

It took about an hour of steady climbing around 9,000 feet altitude just to reach their elevation. The goats were feeding upwards across precipitous cliffs. For another hour I clambered toward them. My heart was thundering in my chest. My pulse was pounding in my ears. Sweat stood out in droplets over my face, neck and arms. Only the cool flow of snow air gave relief. I took great risks pulling myself up from ledge to ledge.

Closer and closer I squirmed toward the three wild mountain goats. Slowly the distance between us was being narrowed down. Now it was less than fifty feet and they did not even detect I was on their range. This was a moment of wonderful solitude, of supreme satisfaction—an aged man on a remote mountain in close company with three of his wild friends of black hooves and white hair. After almost another hour of gentle approach I shot the last picture at less than twenty feet. I came down off those granite crags a man renewed and rejuvenated beyond human language to express.

Just last summer I decided to explore a mountain range I had never been in before. It was tough terrain, and just by my Father's gentle guidance I pushed my way into a wilderness clearing where I could camp safely. I was preparing a simple supper when a large she-wolf appeared at the forest edge alone. I began to follow her at once. I was sure she must have a den in the dense timber. There I lost her tracks in the deep undergrowth.

I returned to my camp, ate supper in silence, then prepared my primitive bed for the night. Suddenly, just at sundown; the setting sun came out from a dark cloud bank. Wondrous golden light filled the whole clearing. It etched every tree, blade of grass and rough stone in exquisite detail.

Suddenly a huge male wolf, the largest and most handsome specimen I had ever seen, stepped out of the timber into the full glory of the sunset. His beautiful tawny coat rippled as if woven from spun gold. My breathing almost stopped as he circled my camp. Closer and closer he came! A magnificent look of intelligence, dignity and good will filled his eyes. Finally he was only about fifty feet from me, standing there in solitary splendor.

Satisfied I meant him no harm, he moved off into the forest where the female had gone. A great grin creased my face. What a spectacle! What an unforgettable interlude! What joy! Thank You, Father, for such a rare treasure no one can take from me.

At dawn the next day I moved quietly up the mountain valley. The woods were full of wild fruit, borne in abundance upon the vigorous undergrowth of the forest. I revelled in the luscious flavor of wild Huckleberries, Blueberries, Thimbleberries, and Sallal Berries. It surprised me that I did not run into any bears banqueting on the wild fruit, though their trails were evidence of their presence.

Softly I came to a singing mountain stream. It fanned out in wide riffles over a glistening sand bar. I sat down quietly to listen to its song and to inhale deeply of the perfume from co-mingled pine, spruce and fir. Then there stepped from the shadows of the trees a handsome doe and her twin fawns. They stood silently in the morning sunlight, soaking up its warmth. Soon the first doe was joined by a second, also with twins, then a third with her dappled, spotted offspring.

It was a scene of supreme serenity. Nine deer at the water's edge, each of them reflected in the shining surface. After testing the wind they stepped into the stream to slake their thirst. Then, as if by a prearranged plan, all of them began to prance around and play in the shallows on the sand bar. It was a beautiful ballet with droplets of water and sheets of silver spray flung from their feet in sun-spangled artistry.

There I sat, still as a stone, and witnessed one of the most exquisite pageantries ever seen in the wild. It lasted but a few minutes, yet its impact and beauty were etched so deeply upon my memory they will never be forgotten.

Such moments are precious, rare and beyond any human measurement. For me they are lovely bonuses bestowed by my Father in abundance. To Him I am ever grateful for His loving generosity and gentle affection.

Chapter 19

Ever Wider Horizons

The advancing years of our sojourn in the north were not just taken up with mountain exploration. Elsewhere I have written at length about our personal interaction with various families and dear friends who faced death. Already mention has been made of our new insight into the dreadful drug traffic that destroys so many lives and wrecks so many homes. But beyond all these was an even wider outreach arranged by our Father to touch the hearts of men and women in Christian leadership roles.

First it should be mentioned that increasingly I have been given a special sense of acute responsibility to pray for our leaders. As one's age increases and correspondingly his strength diminishes, there still remains the grand honor and noble pleasure of praying for others. It is the most worthwhile enterprise in which any elderly person can invest his or her time. It demands time; it calls for thoughtful concentration; it requires strength of spirit and solitude of soul, in company with Christ.

In my case, three special areas of concern have been laid upon me by God's Gracious Spirit. Most recently a fourth has been added. These are quite simply: Leadership in government at all levels both at home and abroad. Leadership in the church world-wide. Leadership in every form of media. Leadership in education everywhere.

For me as a common man living in rather remote places, without any artificial attempts to generate public acclaim or national attention, it has been thrilling to see our Father at work in His world. Those humble prayers of intense intercession offered in the wondrous name and authority of His Majesty—The Living Christ—have been answered. God has been pleased to move in wondrous ways His purposes to fulfill upon the planet.

It is not unusual for those of us who have a wide grasp of history to be apprehensive about the social decline and degrading decadence of our society. We are not blind to the formidable dangers of our corrupt culture. Nor are we immune to the terrible trauma of our times, where moral decay consumes us as a cancer.

If we are people of intellectual integrity and deep spiritual perception we will not be deceived nor deluded by the superficiality of the modern world. We will not be lulled into an easy accommodation with those who would have us believe that all is well in our contemporary society. It is not! There are great perils on every side, especially for God's people. Our part is to be awake, alert and active in the work to which Christ calls us.

The challenges facing Christ's followers today are not being adequately addressed by the twentieth century church. There are predators in many of our pulpits. Christ Himself calls us to be bold and brave on His behalf. His church is being seduced by a soft and self-indulgent culture. For those of us who care deeply there is but one final line of defense. It is the eternal majesty and might of The Most High Himself. He is our great shield, our defender, our victor! Only to Him can we turn in our extremity.

This is the role of prayer and intercession. It is a role neglected by many elderly people. In our age of relative affluence and ease, too often these people are too busy playing golf and bridge, cruising tropical seas or freeways, to be bothered with the burdens of a broken world. Who wants to think about broken homes, broken careers, broken dreams or broken children? It's much more fun to play games; play the slot machines; play the casinos; play pool; or just simply play the fool.

Still in every era of human history our Father has His own small, special remnant of chosen people, whom He has chosen and called to be His intercessors. To these He entrusts the heavy responsibility to be His own ambassadors. He calls them into profound sacrificial intercession for a perishing world, and He sends them out with tear-stained eyes and sobbing cries to warn men and women everywhere of their imminent peril.

This is no easy calling. For as is well known, if we are intensely earnest in our prayers for change, God will, more often than not, call upon us to be the agents of His appointment to answer and fulfill those very self-same prayers. We will become an integral part of the practical response to our own petitions.

Certainly this was true for me. Little did I ever dream that as an ordinary lay person I would be called upon to address whole conferences assembled for professional clergy. It was a terrifying assignment to take on. Like some of the ancient prophets of old, it seemed a formidable task to tackle. After all, why should or would they even listen to me? I had neither the academic credentials nor polished oratory of the professional person, to command a hearing or attract acclaim from a cynical audience of professional leaders.

Still those were the assignments given to me by my Father. I went in trembling. But my confidence reposed in Christ. He was my Commander. I was a man under His authority, His messenger sent with clear instructions from Himself. Whether or not His orders were carried out was not my responsibility. Each hearer would one day have to report why he had responded as he did. My part was simply to be faithful as Christ's servant to deliver His Word.

The places I went astonished me. Groups of all sorts from various denominations received the Word from the Most High, some to honor, others to dishonor.

I am aware that it is common in Christian work for those engaged in it to look for tangible results. We are a success-oriented society. We measure a man's worth by the numbers he commands and the net returns delivered. But no such measurement can be used in assessing spiritual achievement. Our Father does not deal in digits. His chief concern is the solitary inner response of a single soul to the still quiet voice of His Spirit. Ultimately He deals with us as individuals. He does not manipulate us en masse. Few people perceive this in our pompous programs.

So it was that in large measure I refused to keep any record of results achieved. I would not be drawn into showing off statistics to try and impress others. As I saw it, my widening horizons were of my Father's design. It was He who now commissioned me to share His truth with all sorts of leaders drawn from a wide variety of backgrounds.

Out of this there emerged a growing and acute awareness that many leaders lead very lonely lives. Many shared with me the inner anguish of their own spirits over the world in which they worked. They gave me the clear and convincing impression that they were weary of trying to use special techniques or polished programs to reach perishing people. What they longed for was, rather, a clear command, a ringing assurance, a living Word from The Living Christ that would renew and refresh them for the fray. It was Christ Himself who must be the dynamic of their lives. He alone could empower them to overcome a corrupt culture. He it was who would enable them to triumph over evil.

From all this there emerged the book, *Predators in Our Pulpits: A Compelling Challenge to Follow Christ in These Perilous Times.* Its message had been on my spirit for years. Now the time had come to deliver it.

Again the question was not, "How many books would sell?"—"Or would this work make the best-seller list?" Rather, the central concern was that it be used by our Father to awaken His people to their peril. Here our faith could not repose in any publisher, editor, sales strategy, bookstore or publicity. Our confidence had to reside in Christ Himself. He it was who could use this little book to change the entire thrust of the contemporary church. His Spirit could use it to help us see the need for sacrificial living amongst God's people. Our Father would be faithful to use it to touch and transform the lives of leaders.

Our quiet trust that this would take place has been invested entirely in Him. I do not rely on public relations, advertising agencies or "hype" in the media to try and advance our Father's work in the world. In His own gentle manner, in His own good time, in His own powerful persistence, He will perform and perfect His purposes. My special pleasure will be to see and wonder at the marvel of His ways. It has always been so. With profound inner sincerity there rises from my spirit the eternal song of praise, "Thank You, Father!"

What applies to this book and to these messages, applies equally to all the other books, tapes and studies. It is His doing, not mine, that now they have reached all over the earth in more than two dozen languages. It is His arrangement that millions upon millions of readers and listeners have come into a closer walk with Christ, a clearer understanding of His will for them, a more intimate awareness of our Father's love.

All this is very heartening, very cheering. Yet amid it all in His lovely way our Father still stoops down to touch our lives in intimate ways that remind me of this truth: The most beautiful bonuses sometimes come from His dear hands in the darkest hours. Let me recount but one.

An unusual invitation had come to address an annual Bible conference in a community that was entirely strange to me. I had never been in the church where I was to speak. I did not know a single person there, not even the pastor. Nor, outwardly, was there anything to encourage one to go. Still, after seeking my Father's wish in the matter, it was clear I should take the services.

The day I arrived the church itself was closed and there was no one at the manse. I parked in the empty parking lot watching the steady rain stream down from a gray, overcast sky. It seemed ages before anyone appeared. The whole place was like a morgue, dead as death. There was no sign of life, not even in the first stranger to show up. They had no idea where the pastor might be, much less any sort of information about the special meetings supposed to begin that evening.

So I waited and waited! The only distraction was the steady drumbeat of raindrops on the roof and hood of my vehicle. Dusk was descending and soon it would be dark, with the deep night of late fall enfolding the bleak, bare parking lot. It was scarcely an exciting start to a series of Bible studies.

That first evening a small knot of curious people straggled into the sanctuary. Most of them appeared jaded and bored with life. So perhaps it would be a change to show up at the sanctuary and hear a new speaker. But amongst those who came was a small lad of five years. He had persuaded his parents that they should bring him along.

That night, for the first time, the wee fellow met the Master in a convincing way. He went home and kneeling by his own bed with his mother beside him he gave himself completely to Christ at his own request.

Day after day as the meetings went on, others came to me quietly after the services ended. Christ had become so real, so living, so present that they were eager to accept His overtures of peace, good will and complete forgiveness. Men and women went out of that place at peace with our Father, at rest in their souls, cleansed from their polluted past.

It was heartening to see God's Gracious Spirit deal in great depth with men and women of all ages, from the very young to the very aged. Without coercion or pressure from any person, they just quietly, eagerly, hopefully came to Christ to find new life in Him.

It was the last morning service when I noticed in the center of the church an elderly man and his wife whom I recognized. He and I had worked together as young men forty-four years before during the war. He had been a rough, tough character, discharged from the army because of massive wounds to his head and hands. At that time, too, I was a bold young buck intent only on getting ahead in the world. We had not seen each other for years.

When the service ended all the people left the sanctuary except for this couple. I went over to speak to them and found both sobbing quietly. When I approached they lifted faces furrowed with wrinkles, stained with tears, yet radiant with a sublime inner glow. Literally the glory of our God enfolded them!

I took their hands in mine. Words could not convey the profound pathos of my spirit. Then they spoke.

"Never, ever, until this morning, did we know what it meant to truly encounter Christ. He met us here. He has become The Living Lord to us. He has touched us! We will never be the same again. We are His. He is ours!"

When we parted with hearty hugs I could only whisper softly, "Thank You, Father!"

Chapter 20

No Room in the Inn

After a number of years in the mountains with their dry, brisk climate, it was apparent that Ursula's health had improved. She no longer had the severe tendonitis pains in her arms, shoulders and back. For this we were humbly grateful to our Father.

About this time a friend invited us to spend several months in her home down on the coast. It was mid-winter and the difference between the balmy weather of Victoria by the sea and our mountain chalet buried under snow, and sheathed in ice, was startling indeed. We had almost forgotten how pleasant it could be, even if it was rather rainy, to be where warm sea breezes tempered by the ocean currents made it possible for Rhododendron and Primulas to bloom in January.

The best part was the building in which our friend's condominium was located. It was beautifully warm. A magnificent hot water system circulated heat throughout the entire structure of steel and concrete, keeping it at a comfortable, even, healthy temperature. We both felt fit and energetic in this location by the sea, adjacent to a splendid big park whose rolling acres ran down to the sea edge.

Much to my delight I could work here with enormous energy. It was possible to devote much more attention to creative writing in this environment where one was free from fighting with snow, ice and frost, as we had to do up in the mountains.

So we began to wonder if the time had come for us to return to the coast. We prayed earnestly about this. Prices for property seemed prohibitive. We were told it was unlikely we could ever purchase in our friend's location since any units available were immediately taken by local residents.

Rather than becoming anxious and agitated about this matter, we decided quietly to place the issue in our Father's care. If He wished to have us move again, He could open the way for us. We were His children and in His care. In her gentle, quiet confidence Ursula said to me one afternoon, "If He wants us to live here, He could easily send someone to our door who wants to sell their suite!" My reply was just as certain and equally affirmative, "Of course He could! Let's just leave it in His hands!"

Just three days later that was exactly what happened. I was out taking a brisk hike in the winter wind. When I came home Ursula was excited. A stranger and his wife had come to the door to ask if perchance we might be interested in purchasing their unit. It was even more attractive than the one we occupied. There were wide, unobstructed views from its great windows looking out over the park, over the Straits of Juan de Fuca, over the snow-draped Olympics, over the harbor entrance to the rocky Sooke Hills beyond. From its balcony we could watch sunrise and sunset.

Just the night before they had decided to sell after living there for fourteen years. There was one catch. We had to decide that night whether to purchase or not, since their granddaughter was a real estate agent who would list it the next day, if we did not take it. A further factor was the price. As vendors sometimes do, they wanted us to make them an offer on the unit.

Asking for several hours to reach a decision, we sought guidance from our Father. The clear conviction given to me was that we should not submit an offer. Rather, we established in mind clearly the price we could afford to pay without incurring any debts. If that was matched by the seller it was the place prepared for us by our Father. So we returned that evening in excited expectation.

Briefly I put it to the owners in this way: "You are elderly people in the twilight of life. You know exactly what price you must be paid to cover your needs. Simply state it. If we can meet it we will. The simple answer will be 'yes' or 'no.'"

The response was immediate. The gentleman quoted a figure much lower than we had even hoped for. My "*Yes,* we will take it!" brought broad smiles to all of our faces. Everyone was satisfied and happy. That very evening in a remarkable way the whole transaction was completed, since the owner had himself been a former real estate agent.

The next morning a notary public confirmed that the sale was satisfactory. For the remarkably modest charge of only $25.00 the deal was completed. We were the ecstatic owners of a lovely little suite high in the sky. In such a simple yet startling sequence of events we had been provided with a place to reside when others said in effect, "There is no room in the Inn." But there was for us, within our Father's gentle care.

What was perhaps equally astonishing was the price itself. After the sale was completed the owner disclosed to us that he had been offered $20,000.00 more for the condominium just a few months before. But he was not then ready to sell. So in truth the arrangement of the transaction was convincing evidence of our Father's concern for us. How dear and trustworthy He is!

The question now came up, "What about 'Chalet Sunshine'?" We certainly did not want to own two homes. But before deciding to sell it we felt it was wise to wait awhile to be doubly sure the cool coastal climate would not cause Ursula's tendonitis to recur. Little did we dream what incredible events the next few months would produce in our lives. Yet each was to be a part of our Father's plan.

That summer turned out to be the hottest and driest in more than a decade. British Columbia's vast mountain ranges were like a tinderbox. The forests and rangeland flared with ferocious fires. Millions of acres went up in smoke, reduced to ashes and the stark, dark skeletons of burned trees.

I went up to "Chalet Sunshine" to pick up my camper. The day I arrived scattered plumes of smoke from bush fires were rising in the hills around our home. At first they seemed so small, so inoffensive. But by dark a stiff west wind had fanned them into a blazing inferno. This, coupled with rising daytime temperatures well over 100°, had suddenly produced fierce updrafts that took the firestorm up the slopes and across the country in wild abandon.

The forestry fire fighting crews threw all the resources they could into the fray. Water bombers roared overhead. Water-hauling helicopters thundered into the hills. Huge D-8 bulldozers scoured a formidable firebreak over the rocky terrain. Hundreds of bone-weary, smoke-blackened fire fighters tried to hold back the advancing flames. In the night it raged across the rangeland, blackening over 4,000 acres. It roared through the forest, its heat exploding into giant flames that leaped up the hills in ferocious anger.

It appeared our little cluster of fourteen homes tucked away in the hills would be burned to the ground. We were warned to remove all our valuables and be ready to evacuate at any moment.

In quietness of spirit I spoke softly to my Father: "It was You who led me to this spot. It was You who supplied us with this home. It is Yours! You can preserve it if You so wish. Or You may choose to remove it from our care. Whatever You decide, it is agreeable with me."

Then in the quiet assurance that all was well I laid down and slept soundly—probably the only person in the community to do so.

At dawn the fires had burned down to gray ash. The flames came to within 100 yards of the nearest building. But not a single structure had been ignited. The whole countryside, except the golf course in front of the house, was black and gray, stark and dark. There was not a soul stirring. I went out to walk amid the desolation. For me, as a passionate lover of the wild and beautiful land, this landscape was as barren and bleak as any angry, ravaged battle field. No longer could I live amid those fire-blackened hills.

"Chalet Sunshine," it seemed, had lost half its worth. No one, surely, would ever want a home in such a stark setting. So I locked the door and drove away, wondering what would ever happen to our happy home in the hills.

Late that summer I suddenly felt a strong urge to call an agent to sell the place. His response was the it was well-nigh hopeless. No one would want the house now! But to satisfy me he would try.

He was told of a family who several years before had shown interest in the area. But they lived in Alberta, some 500 miles away, and all his attempts to reach them proved futile. At least he would go up and stick a "For Sale" sign in the rockery in front of the lonely house. It was sort of a hopeless gesture, but it might placate this persistent owner who was so sure now was the time to sell.

As he stood in the yard pushing the "FOR SALE" sign into the rocky ground, he was being watched by a couple playing golf on the green in front of the house. They dropped their clubs, rushed across the road excitedly and asked to see the house. It was exactly what they wanted! They were the couple from Alberta on holiday, whom the agent had been unable to contact!

Without a qualm they quietly paid us the new price we had asked, all cash, with request to take possession in fifteen days. In less than three days the whole transaction was completed. Nor did we lose a cent. Such is the gentle wonder of our Father's loving concern.

These events have been recounted here not only to bring honor and respect and gratitude to our Father, but also to encourage my readers to entrust Him with their affairs. More than this, may you discover the great adventure of living in His company.

What has been true for us in the purchase and sale of our various homes, has been equally exciting in our travels across thousands and thousands of mountain miles. Just one incident will be recounted here. Because of its haunting beauty it will also serve as a suitable ending to this book.

Ursula and I had driven hard all day through pouring rain and gusting winds. Our little camper was tossed about in the rough weather like a small sailboat in a stormy sea. Yet we pushed on because we were sure by dark we would reach a sheltered campsite on the California coast.

We pulled into the place worn out, weary and spent with fatigue. Darkness was just falling as I went out into the pouring rain to hook up our power and water lines for the night. Just then the camp director sent out his young lady assistant to tell us we could not stay. He insisted that his camp policy was such that we had to push on to the next location more than 100 miles farther down the road.

For us this was impossible. We were done for the day. I had been at the wheel for more than twelve hours in terrible driving conditions. Not knowing what to do we drove disconsolately out onto the highway. I recalled a side road which led down to a motel that might provide shelter. Seeing some bright lights in the winter gloom I pulled up next to the office only to discover we were at a brand new lodge built on the sea edge.

At my urging, Ursula went in to see what she could do. A few moments later she returned to say the desk clerk had been very courteous, took pity on us and would provide a room at a reasonable rate. So would I please go in to the office, register the vehicle and pay for our overnight stay in this very posh place?

I almost hesitated to go in. My clothes were dripping wet and I was disheveled. My eyes were red, bloodshot from straining to see through the rain-splashed windows. I had not shaved for two days. My boots squelched water. I really did look like a tramp from the wrong side of town. But I went in!

The young lady behind the front desk took a long, tender, knowing look at me then spoke softly: "Your wife told me how the camp manager forced you out on the road tonight. *No Room in the Inn?* I've seen it again and again. I used to work in these camps!"

A grin crossed my grizzled features. I was glad we had found someone who understood. Quietly I filled out the registration form. The girl stood staring at my bedraggled figure. Then she spoke again: "You are not to turn another wheel tonight. Leave your camper right where it is. I have decided to make you our special houseguests for tonight. I am giving you our choicest suite. You will even be provided with a full, free breakfast in our ocean view dining room!"

It seemed too good to be true! I was dazed with delight. When she opened the door to the special guest suite words failed me. Its open ceilings soared twenty feet to huge skylights. Not only was there a magnificent big bed, but also a full couch, easy chairs and a huge fireplace. "Light the logs!" she chuckled. "Live it up! Let's go for it!" What a warm welcome for two weary wanderers.

We pulled back the curtains and there in full view the ocean thundered and roared on the rocks beneath us. What a spectacle—what a superb setting! In the midst of utter desolation and dejection our Father had brought us to this place of refuge and rest. Like His angel in disguise He had prepared this dear girl to do us so much good.

All this lingers on in our memories of His never-failing faithfulness to us, His feeble children. How gracious, how generous! Thank You, Father!!

Chapter 21

The Fabric of Faith in God

There are seven strands to the fabric of our faith in God, our Father. They are absolutely basic to living with Him in joyous good will. It requires a clear understanding of how these are each interwoven into our intimate interrelationship with Him in order to revel in His companionship and rest quietly in His remarkable care for us.

1. Discover First Hand the Living Reality of God.

It is imperative on our part to seek Him. It is not that He is a remote and distant deity wrapped in mystical obscurity. He is not! He is here! Our human hindrance is that we are so entangled in the trappings of our earth sojourn—so conditioned to live only in terms of our five fallible senses and so blinded by our selfish instincts—that we cannot see or perceive His presence next to us, amongst us.

Our arrogant, cynical society insists He does not even exist. Our skeptical scientists assert He cannot be known or proven by the scientific process. Our educators exclude any mention of Him in their classrooms. For most of the common people He is no more than an obscure being, ensconced somewhere far out in the immensity of space. He is a remote power to whom people sometimes appeal in times of extremity or moments of crisis. But He is not their Father, their Friend, their Source of Faith.

In spite of such barriers between Him and us, He in turn comes to us continually. He touches our lives at a thousand turns in our tangled trails. He speaks to us in subtle, sensitive ways by His Gentle Spirit. He woos us with patience through His Word. Through the compassion of Christ He calls us to come to Him. He draws us to discover Him everywhere at work in His wondrous creation:

That they should seek the Lord,
if haply they might feel after him and find him,
though he be not far from every one of us:
For in him we live, and move, and have our being;
as certain also of your own poets have said,
for we are also his offspring (Acts 17:27–28).

But without faith it is impossible to please him:
for he that cometh to God must believe that he is,
and that he is a rewarder of them that diligently seek him (Hebrews 11:6).

2. Come to Know and Respect Him Intimately.

It is not enough to know *about* God in an intellectual, academic or theoretical manner. He is not just an historical figure or a theological curiosity. Nor is He a fantastic fabrication of man's imagination.

Rather, He is a living being. He is a person who can be known by man. He possesses a personality which experiences all the emotions familiar to us human beings . . . be they joy, grief, anger or compassion. He owns the most remarkable mind in the cosmos. He has a breadth of understanding exceeding anything ever imagined by our greatest thinkers. His character is impeccable in its integrity, justice, compassion and generosity.

He has no equals, no peers, no similar associates. Yet in His incredible concern for us earthlings, whom He deigns to call "His children," He lovingly calls us to Himself. He invites us to invest our confidence in Him. He asks us to capitulate to His legitimate claims upon us—to respond in quiet trust to the integrity of His character, and to reciprocate a little of the enormous love He bestows on us.

To help us humans do this He has come to us in human guise through the Person of His Son. It is Christ who is the visible expression of the Invisible God. In Him we can see clearly the true character of our Father. And, wonder of wonders, it is through Him that we can come to know His Father as *our* Father, or even better, *my* Father.

Through Christ's perfect life, perfect death, perfect resurrection, perfect restoration to power in the universe, we too can partake of His eternal life. It is He who sets us free from our enslavement to sin, to self, to Satan. We are set free to follow Christ, to keep company with Him, to gradually know God as our Father, our Friend, our Confidante.

It is this intimate interchange between Him and us that imparts His eternal life, His love, His illumination to us:

> *And this is life eternal,*
> *that they might know thee the only true God,*
> *and Jesus Christ, whom thou hast sent* (John 17:3).

> *Therefore if any man be in Christ,*
> *he is a new creature: old things are passed away;*
> *behold, all things are become new.*

And all things are of God,
who hath reconciled us to himself by Jesus Christ,
and hath given to us the ministry of reconciliation (2 Corinthians 5:17–18).

3. In Loyalty and Gratitude, Love and Obey Him.

As we begin to share life with our Father, we find springing up within us an enormous outflow of gratitude for His generosity to us. All of life takes on a totally new dimension of delight and dignity. We discover our true identity in our dynamic relationship to God as our Father. He is near, He is dear, He is clear to our view. We find fulfillment, acceptance, worth and inner integrity as His children. We become acutely aware that He knows us intimately, understands us fully, deals with us in loving concern and has only our best interests in view.

All of this ever-expanding awareness begins to generate a personal, positive response on my part. In turn there is born within me a new spirit. There is created within my soul a new aspiration to please Him, to live for Him, to comply with His wishes, to do His bidding. This is done spontaneously, joyously, promptly—out of gratitude and love and loyalty. I find it simple to invest my confidence, my trust, my faith in Him, for He is so totally trustworthy.

This loyalty and love for my Father has its origin in Him. I love Him because He first loved me and gave Himself for me. It is not a drudgery but rather a delight to do His will. I do not wish to live in opposition or rebellion to His good and noble purposes for me. Rather, it is a high honor to have a significant part in seeing them accomplished upon the planet.

Such simple, straightforward obedience and trust in compliance with His clear instructions brings Him enormous pleasure. He searches for souls who cheerfully align their wills with His. He honors such humble faith in action with innumerable benefits and remarkable blessing. Life with Him becomes a great adventure replete with joy and strength:

> *He that hath my commandments, and keepeth them,*
> *he it is that loveth me:*
> *and he that loveth me shall be loved of my Father,*
> *and I will love him,*
> *and will manifest myself to him* (John 14:21).

> *If a man love me, he will keep my words:*
> *and my Father will love him, and we will come*
> *unto him, and make our abode with him* (John 14:23).

> *If ye abide in me, and my words abide in you,*
> *ye shall ask what ye will,*
> *and it shall be done unto you.*
> *Herein is my Father glorified,*
> *that ye bear much fruit: so shall ye be my disciples.*
> *As the Father hath loved me,*
> *so have I loved you:*
> *continue ye in my love* (John 15:7–9).

4. *Serve Him and Others First and Faithfully.*

The capacity to trust our Father in calm faith is a gracious gift which He Himself bestows on us. It is not a faculty of our minds nor an exercise of our emotions—nor even a determination of our wills, though each of these three attributes of our souls is brought into action as we live by faith in God. Basically, calm confidence in the character of our Father, that He will make good His commitments to us, comes from the very life and person of Christ Himself who takes command in any life turned over to His authority.

Christ does not dispense His faith to me for my personal advantage apart from Himself. Rather, it is His faith imparted to me continuously by His residence within me that enables me to trust my Father implicitly. It is His faith shared with me by His Gracious Spirit in me that exercises total, unflinching trust in God. This capacity to invest calm confidence in Him is not given to me for selfish purposes or personal show of power or prestige. It is to please Him, to serve His purposes and to enrich His people.

As with love for God, so likewise with faith in God, its function is to honor Him first and bless others secondly. In so doing, my own life is enhanced beyond belief, and wondrous things are accomplished in the economy of God. Our Father does not reward faith to bring attention to my little life. He honors faith to demonstrate His Own utter integrity and total trustworthiness. Through the simple exercise of obedient faith by His children He shows to all the world how faithful He is as our Father!

God Himself is the source of faith. He produces it. He exercises it. He imparts it to those of us who share His life. In essence it is my personal, positive, private response to His character and to His Word, to the point where I act in obedience. And, because of His impeccable character and unbreakable promises, this faith is vindicated because it is invested in Him. He validates it!

But seek ye first the kingdom of God,
and his righteousness;
And all these things shall be added unto you
(Matthew 6:33).

Verily, verily, I say unto you,
he that believeth on me, the works that I do
shall he do also; and greater works than these
shall he do; because I go unto my Father.
And whatsoever ye shall ask in my name,
that will I do, that the Father may be glorified in the Son.
If ye shall ask anything in my name, I will do it (John 14:12–14).

5. Declare, Boldly and Openly, Confidence in Christ.

When God, our Father, becomes the central figure in our affairs; when Christ, our Most High Majesty, yet dearest Friend, assumes control of our character and conduct; when God's Gracious Spirit, our Counselor, guides our decisions and leads us in the paths of wholesomeness, we may be confident all is well. We can face the most formidable misfortune, taste the deepest sorrow or walk through the utmost darkness—because our confidence is in God.

The clear, categorical command given to us by Christ when He was here was *"have faith in God."* To do this daily, diligently, requires our genuine devotion to Him. It demands that without apology, display or embarrassment we state openly and boldly our unshakeable loyalty and confidence in Him. It is He who achieves His good purposes in our lives. He is able to accomplish in us far more than we might otherwise ever expect. He can bring great good out of even the most grievous setbacks.

This life of calm trust in Christ is not without its tough times and dark days. He warned us it would be so. But amid the turmoil of our times we can be people of good cheer and great courage, for He is with us. It is He who overcomes the obstacles. It is He who sustains our strength amid the stresses and strains of life. He is our assurance, our hope, our life. He is here!

Without fanfare or ostentation we should declare aloud our awareness of His presence with us. Let all those around us know it is He who supplies our courage and undergirds our will to carry on. Our faith does not repose in man, his technical ingenuity or human resources! It rests in the unchangeable goodness of our Father—God, very God!!

> *Have not I commanded thee?*
> *Be strong and of a good courage; be not afraid, neither be thou dismayed: for the Lord thy God is with thee whithersoever you goest* (Joshua 1:9).

> . . . *Your faith should not stand in the wisdom of men, but in the power of God* (1 Corinthians 2:5).

6. Praise and Honor God Continually. Please Him with Child-Like Trust.

In the implicit interaction between Father and child more than bare obedience is essential. There must come the compelling joy of finding deep delight in His company. Over and over our Father fills our little lives with the overflowing abundance of His bounties. He enfolds us in His great strong arms of love. He pours into our souls a song of serenity!

In all of this our spirits become acutely aware that it is He who gives exquisite purpose to our few years on the planet. It is He who brings gentle dignity into our days. He is our Father, we are His children. In His care we need not be alarmed or dismayed. He it is who leads us by the hand, whispering softly: "This is the way. Walk in it with assurance."

This intimate relationship between Him and us can be far more precious, more compelling, more uplifting than even the finest human interaction because He is utterly reliable! And since our faith has found its delightful resting place in Him there arises from our souls a joyous hymn of praise and adoration to His unchanging faithfulness.

It is our inner attitude of gratitude which brings such satisfaction to our Father. When our lives are in truth a litany of love and appreciation for Him, He is overjoyed. He delights to do for us far more than we could have imagined. The praise, the honor, the respect we bestow upon Him by our childlike confidence is the most precious praise we can give Him.

It is this sweet interaction between Him and us that makes our walk with Him through this world so precious. It is He who leads us by still waters and into green pastures. It is He who in gentle kindness enriches our days with His care.

Bless the Lord, O my soul:
and all that is within me,
bless his holy name.
Bless the Lord, O my soul,
and forget not all his benefits:
who forgiveth all thine iniquities;
who healeth all thy diseases;
who redeemeth thy life from destruction;
who crowneth thee with lovingkindness
and tender mercies;
who satisfieth thy mouth with good things;
so that thy youth is renewed like the eagle's
(Psalm 103:1–5).

Be careful for nothing; but in every thing
by prayer and supplication with thanksgiving
let your requests be made known unto God.

> *And the peace of God, which passeth all understanding, shall keep your hearts and minds through Christ Jesus* (Philippians 4:6–7).

7. *In Humility, Be Still and Rest in Him. Wait Quietly for His Time.*

Our faith in our Father is not something to boast about. We do not hold it up as a stunning display of our special spirituality. It is not some unusual mark of honor or badge of merit we flaunt before others. Rather, this element in our lives is seen as a very private, precious gift bestowed upon us by the generosity of Christ. Even if it be as minute as a single grain of mustard seed, it is viable and vibrant because of the glorious character of the One in whom it is invested. He it is who vindicates our confidence in Himself.

When we understand this basic truth it humbles us before Him. We come to see that it is His faithfulness to us that validates our childlike trust. And in this awareness of His enduring goodness we are still before Him, quiet in repose, resting in His eternal kindness. There is no place here for pride or pretense. We are at peace, and that sublime inner stillness has its source and serenity in Him.

As the Spirit of God states so emphatically again and again, "We are to abide in Him, while He, in turn, abides in us!" There is an intimate, personal interrelationship of such a caliber that our rest, our assurance, our strength all repose in Him. He is in me, and I am in Him. In His own good time and in His own unique way He accomplishes His own good purposes in my little life. I am His and He is mine forever and forever. What a sublime and wondrous assurance!

The intense, moving, stirring awareness that God is my Father, that I am His child, transcends every other consideration in life. What a special privilege! In quietness, in contentment, in gentle rest I bow my spirit and whisper: "Thank You, Father!"

> *Be still, and know that I am God:*
> *I will be exalted among the heathen,*
> *I will be exalted in the earth.*
> *The Lord of hosts is with us;*
> *the God of Jacob is our refuge. Selah* (Psalm 46:10–11).

> *There remaineth therefore a rest*
> *to the people of God.*
> *For he that is entered into his rest,*
> *he also hath ceased from his own works,*
> *as God did from his* (Hebrews 4:9–10).